gluten-free, vegan cooking
IN YOUR
instant pot®

gluten-free, vegan cooking
IN YOUR
instant pot®

65 DELICIOUS WHOLE FOOD RECIPES
FOR A PLANT-BASED DIET

kathy hester

BESTSELLING AUTHOR OF
THE ULTIMATE VEGAN COOKBOOK FOR YOUR INSTANT POT

PAGE STREET
PUBLISHING CO.

PAGE STREET
PUBLISHING CO.

First published in 2020 by
Page Street Publishing Co.
27 Congress Street, Suite 105
Salem, MA 01970
www.pagestreetpublishing.com

Distributed by Macmillan, sales in Canada by The Canadian Manda Group.

24 23 22 21 20   1 2 3 4 5

ISBN-13: 978-1-62414-946-7
ISBN-10: 1-62414-946-4

Library of Congress Control Number: 2019905873

Cover and book design by Kylie Alexander for Page Street Publishing Co.
Photography by Kathy Hester

Printed and bound in China

Instant Pot® is a registered trademark of Double Insight, Inc. which was not involved in the creation of this book.

Dedication

I want to dedicate this book to you, my reader, for all of your support. I also want to dedicate this book to all of my friends and testers who make it possible for me to create a cookbook like this. I can't thank you all enough. I can't leave out my elder dog, Brenna, as she spent as much time in the kitchen as I did!

table of contents

Introduction

I'm Kathy Hester, and I run PlantBasedInstantPot.com and HealthySlowCooking.com. I also have a free private Facebook group called Vegan Recipes: Cooking with Kathy Hester. This is my tenth cookbook, and I love creating easy recipes that you can adapt to use what you have on hand or to fit your particular diet.

I believe wholeheartedly that you can eat amazing food no matter what your dietary limitations or preferences are!

The Ultimate Vegan Cookbook for Your Instant Pot® was my first electric pressure cooker cookbook, and it started me on my Instant Pot obsession. I love the way that you can cook things at the last minute, make beans without soaking them or cooking them for hours, and you can do it all without heating up your house in the summer.

Be sure to follow my Facebook page, Plant-Based Instant Pot®, to see videos of me demoing Instant Pot recipes, or you can watch live and ask questions in real time.

I've also written several other vegan cookbooks, including:

- *The Revised Vegan Slow Cooker*
- *The Great Vegan Bean Book*
- *Vegan Slow Cooking for Two or Just You*
- *OATrageous Oatmeals*
- *The Easy Vegan Cookbook*
- *The Ultimate Vegan Cookbook for Your Instant Pot®*
- *Vegan Cooking in Your Air Fryer*
- *The Ultimate Vegan Cookbook*

Why Write a Gluten-Free Cookbook?

I've always provided gluten-free options in my cookbooks, but gluten-free cooking became more personal last year. I was diagnosed with a gluten allergy by my doctor, and it was confirmed by a test.

I thought I would take it in stride, but I was so upset as I went through my pantry and gave away boxes of things that contained gluten that I had been saving for a special occasion. Honestly, this shocked me because I already knew the basics of gluten-free cooking.

For me, the detox process was particularly hard and affected me emotionally the most. Gluten can actually be addictive to some of us that can't tolerate it, and I was one of those lucky few. It took a few months to get through it, but now I feel better than ever.

I don't think every person needs to eat gluten-free, but these gluten-free recipes can be enjoyed by everyone in your household. Once you have a specialty gluten-free flour blend you like, some gluten-free soy sauce and a little initiative, you'll be eating your old favorites in no time.

What Gluten-Free Flour Blends Do I Use?

All the recipes calling for a gluten-free baking blend have been tested with Krusteaz Gluten Free All Purpose Flour and Bob's Red Mill 1-to-1 Baking Flour. They both use similar ingredients, but Bob's Red Mill is much easier to get and you can find it in most grocery stores.

If you prefer a different blend, feel free to use it—just know that you may need to add a little xanthan gum if your blend does not contain it. Xanthan gum keeps your gluten-free baked goods from crumbling. Both the tested blends for this book have it.

Also note that some blends contain whole grains and others don't; you may find yourself needing to add a little more liquid or flour depending on what you use.

How Do I Watch Out for Hidden Gluten?

Some ingredients, such as wheat flour, seitan, barley, wheat berries and the like, are easy to avoid. Some things you might not expect to have gluten—but they do.

If you weren't a label reader before, now is the time to start. Check the allergen list to get a quick idea of whether a product could be okay. Then read the ingredients list carefully to make sure the product is vegan and that it doesn't have hidden wheat flour or gluten in it.

SOY SAUCE, TAMARI AND OTHER ASIAN BOTTLED SAUCES

Be sure these products are clearly marked gluten-free! I've been able to find gluten-free soy sauce, tamari, hoisin sauce, teriyaki sauce and more.

Tamari definitely needs a label check. Many brands are wheat-free. Others contain wheat, and some were once wheat-free but now have added wheat. Products change, companies change and new brands come on the market—it pays to read the labels.

Check anything that contains soy sauce, such as bottled teriyaki sauce. There are a few brands that make gluten-free sauces. You can find them at Whole Foods, health food stores or look online. You can also substitute coconut aminos for soy sauce.

ALL YEASTS ARE NOT GROWN THE SAME WAY

Nutritional yeast is gluten-free, but most brewer's yeast has been grown from spent yeast and is usually contaminated with gluten-containing grains.

Yeast extract can go either way. If you see yeast extract listed in the ingredients, I recommend that you check to see if the product is marked gluten-free.

GLUTENY GRAINS

Avoid bulgur, barley, spelt, Kamut, semolina, triticale, rye, wheat, wheat germ and wheat berries. They all naturally contain gluten.

OATS NEED TO BE LABELED GLUTEN-FREE!

Some grains don't naturally contain gluten, but are often cross-contaminated during harvesting. This happens with oats a lot. It's easy to find and order gluten-free rolled oats, steel-cut oats and oat groats from online stores.

SPICES AND SPICE BLENDS

Most spices and spice blends are gluten-free. I still recommend that you always read the labels—even for spices. Some spices, such as hing or asafoetida, are commonly ground with wheat flour. You can always buy these on Amazon if you can't find them locally. Just be sure to read the ingredients and to search "gluten-free asafoetida" so you only look through the ones that meet your needs.

The same advice goes with Jamaican curry powder. I was surprised that the most popular blend on Amazon had wheat, but I was able to find another that was gluten-free. There's also a recipe in this book to make your own gluten-free Jamaican curry powder (page 53).

NOT GLUTEN-FREE?

You do not need to eat a gluten-free diet to find some treasures in this book. In fact, you can even do the opposite of what my other books suggest and substitute whole wheat pastry flour where a gluten-free baking blend is called for. You will enjoy these recipes gluten-free or not!

Welcome to Your Instant Pot

WHAT IS AN INSTANT POT OR ELECTRIC PRESSURE COOKER?

An Instant Pot® is basically a multicooker, which means it has functions to cook multiple ways. That would be the end of the description except that not all multicookers are the same. I know, it's confusing.

The bottom line is some multicookers do not have a pressure cooker setting. For example, the Instant Pot brand's Aura and Gem models are *not* the multicookers that we are using in this book.

In this book, and most books written for an Instant Pot, the pressure cooker function is the one most used. Instant Pot calls the genre we want *pressure multicookers*. There are similar versions from Ninja®, KitchenAid® and more, so make sure there is a pressure cooker function on any one that you purchase.

Please note that Instant Pot® is the registered trademark of Double Insight Inc., and that Instant Pot was designed in Canada, with healthy living, green living and ethnic diversity in mind.

WHY USE AN INSTANT POT?

I love my electric pressure cooker. If you've been using yours for any time at all I bet you do, too. It lets you cook dry beans and whole grains in minutes—and even that cooking time is hands-off. That means you can do chores, take a walk or just sit on the deck and read a book as your meal cooks.

An electric pressure cooker is an affordable addition to your kitchen. They are on sale several times a year on Amazon and in brick-and-mortar stores, too. Depending on the size, brand and model, they vary in price from $60 to more than $200.

An electric pressure cooker is easy to clean up because you can sauté and cook right in the same pan. It's also safer than the old-timey pressure cookers because it has tons of safety features. If stovetop pressure cookers make you nervous, you're safe with your electric pressure cooker.

WHAT ARE THE DIFFERENCES IN MODELS AND BRANDS?

The name Instant Pot is a brand name of an electric pressure cooker, much like Kleenex® is a brand of tissues. Instant Pot is just one of many multicookers you can use. The names may be different, but what you are really looking for is a multicooker with an electric pressure cooker setting. There are new models and brands popping up constantly. They tend to mimic the Instant Pot, because it's the most popular brand.

Each brand may have different wording on the buttons, though many of them are similar across all brands. Right now, the buttons and basic functions of the Instant Pot, Mealthy and GoWise brands are almost exactly the same. They all include many of the same buttons—sauté, steam, pressure cook, slow cook and rice, just to name a few. These are pressure cooker presets with preprogrammed times.

Next, let's talk about models in the Instant Pot brand. Note that older models will have a button labeled manual and on newer models it's labeled pressure cook.

The Instant Pot Lux is the oldest and most affordable model. It is also the only one that doesn't have a yogurt function, low and high pressure and some of the presets that the newer models do. This one will work for you if you are *not* planning on fermenting.

The Instant Pot Duo and Duo Plus are very similar, with just a few different presets between them. I would only get the Duo Plus if it's on sale and less expensive than the Duo. Either one will do everything you need. I use the Duo, and it is the model that I recommend the most.

The Instant Pot Ultra has an all-digital display that navigates completely differently from the other models. The thing you need to consider is that it's expensive, and it doesn't have many new functions. It does have a super-safe way to release the pressure, but honestly it's no reason to pay $50 extra.

At this writing there is another model called the Instant Pot Max. It's the most expensive, and it's also the only one I don't recommend. It cooks under more pressure which will change recipe times. It also has a few new functions, but I don't think it's worth the price increase. It's supposed to do pressure canning, but I'm not seeing any canning organizations or government canning sites endorsing it, so that makes me nervous. There is a sous vide function as well, but it has not been rated well in reviews that I've seen. I personally haven't used one, but I can't justify the expense. With that said, if it's the model you have then use it—just don't can in it until it gets approved by third-party organizations.

WHAT SIZE INSTANT POT IS RIGHT FOR ME?

You can get Instant Pot brand multicookers in 3-quart (3-L), 6-quart (6-L) or 8-quart (8-L) sizes. Other electric pressure cookers come in those sizes and up to 12 quarts (12 L)!

If you're a family of two or three, a 3-quart (3-L) or a 6-quart (6-L) Instant Pot is a good option. A household of four would do great in a 6-quart (6-L) model, and if you are six or more, I'd think about the 8-quart (8-L) Instant Pot.

Of course, this may change depending on your cooking style. For example, if you love batch cooking and freezing for later, an 8-quart (8-L) size may be a better fit for you even if you live alone or with a small family.

Instant Pot in "venting" position.

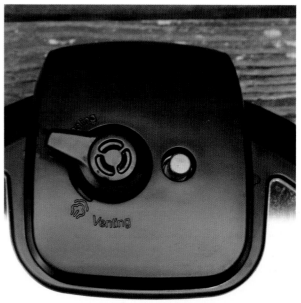

Instant Pot in "sealing" position.

This little stainless steel "cage" protects the Instant Pot from clogging. It also comes off to be cleaned as well.

HOW DO I USE MY INSTANT POT FOR THE VERY FIRST TIME?

Make sure that the area around the pot is clear. The outside will get hot and could melt plastic.

Make sure the area over the steam release handle is clear. This includes your upper cabinets—over time the steam can damage and warp them!

Make sure the steam release valve is clear.

Always check to be sure that the inner liner is in the Instant Pot before adding ingredients. This may seem like a no-brainer, but you wouldn't be the first—or the last—to pour beans or liquid into the outer pot with all the electric components!

To make a recipe, just follow the steps in the directions and add the ingredients to your inner liner. When everything is ready to go, twist the Instant Pot lid on tight. If you are using one of the pressure cooking functions, turn the steam release valve to seal. Follow the cooking and pressure release instructions—your Instant Pot takes care of the rest.

Don't know what to make first? If you're feeling comfortable with your Instant Pot, you might sauté before you pressure cook. If you're feeling a little timid, just put a few cups of water in and pressure cook for 5 minutes and let the pressure release naturally.

TESTING YOUR INSTANT POT AND RELEASING THE PRESSURE

To test that your Instant Pot is working properly, do the traditional water test: Add 2 cups (475 ml) of water to your Instant Pot liner. Put the lid on. Make sure the vent is pointed to seal or sealing. Press the manual or pressure cook button, depending on the make and model that you have. Set it to cook for 5 minutes. If it seals and comes up to pressure, then you're in business.

This is also the perfect time to practice releasing the pressure: Once the cooking stops and it turns to warm, let the Instant Pot naturally release the pressure for 10 minutes. "Let the pressure release naturally" means to do nothing. You just wait for the amount of time called for. If no specific time is given, wait until the float pin comes back down. For this we wait for 10 minutes—and the Instant Pot will count that for us as it stops cooking and starts the keep-warm cycle. From there, carefully move the steam release valve from sealing to venting. Use a pot holder to protect your hand from any additional steam.

INSTANT POT SETTINGS AND BUTTONS REFERENCE

I've heard a lot of people talk about wanting to use more of the buttons on their Instant Pots. Most of the recipes you'll find use the manual or pressure cook button, so you may feel like you're leaving some of that fancy functionality on the table.

All the buttons except the sauté, yogurt and slow cooker settings are actually pressure cooker shortcuts. Even steam is a special version of a pressure cooker setting. I'll explain in more detail, but each button has a preset time and cooking level that you can still adjust manually if you like.

MOST-USED BUTTONS

KEEP WARM/CANCEL

- *Press to cancel current program/cooking selection.*
- *Adjust temperature with the adjust button (less/normal/more).*

By default, the Instant Pot will keep your food warm after the cooking time has elapsed. Time will count up so that you know how long it's been on the keep-warm cycle. When you press the button it will turn the heat off.

You will use the keep warm/cancel button often to end the sauté function before you start your next cooking program, such as pressure cooking added ingredients.

- *Adjust temperature with the adjust button (less/normal/more).*
- *No lid is used with this function.*

This button is used to sauté right in the pot so you don't have extra cleanup. We will use it to cook onions and the like before adding the ingredients that will be finished on the manual or slow cooker settings.

The sauté function can also be used before a pressure cooking cycle to heat the pot so it will come up to pressure more quickly. Plus, you can always use it after a pressure cooking cycle if you want to reduce the amount of liquid left in the pot before serving.

MANUAL OR PRESSURE COOK

- *Adjust cook time in minutes with the + and – buttons.*
- *Adjust temperature with the adjust button (low/high).*
- *Pressure cooking lid is used with this pressure cooking function and the steam release handle will be set to sealing or closed.*

This is the function you will probably find yourself using most often.

TIMER

- *You must select a cooking method, like manual, before you can set the time.*
- *Adjust cook time in minutes with the + and – buttons.*

The timer will count down until it's time to begin cooking. This is a great function to use to make fresh steel-cut oats in the morning. You can have it set to start cooking when you wake up in the morning.

WARNING: Do not put perishable food in the pot without heat for a long period of time. This function is best for doing a plain water and grain mixture if it will be in the pot overnight.

SPECIAL COOKING METHODS

SLOW COOKER

- *Adjust cook time in minutes with the + and – buttons.*
- *Adjust temperature with the adjust button (less/normal/more).*
- *The pressure cooking lid can be used with this function and the steam release handle will be set to venting or open. Or you can purchase the Instant Pot glass lid and use that.*

You may need to adjust your favorite recipes when you start cooking them in your Instant Pot. It tends to cook a little hotter, and you will get less evaporation when you use the pressure cooking lid, even with the valve open.

STEAM

- *Defaults to 10 minutes on high pressure.*
- *Pressing the adjust button changes the time (15 or 30 minutes).*
- *Pressing the + and – buttons will still add and subtract minutes from the time.*

This setting is unique in that it heats at full power for the entire cycle. Because of this you always want to use the rack that came with your Instant Pot or a steamer insert when using this setting. It's great for dumplings and steaming vegetables.

- *Defaults to low pressure.*

This setting is actually fully automatic like a rice cooker, and it will adjust the cooking time depending on how much water and rice you use. That said, it's really for white rice. You'll use the manual or multigrain settings for brown and more exotic types of rice.

YOGURT

- *Defaults to 8 hours.*
- *Pressing the adjust button makes big changes on this setting! It will cycle to boil, a setting to pasteurize homemade nondairy milk before you make yogurt, or to 24 hours.*
- *The pressure cooking lid can be used with this function, and the steam release handle can be open or closed.*
- *Pressing the + and – buttons will still add and subtract hours from the time.*

This just keeps the pot warm enough to allow the culture to multiply. I also use the yogurt default setting for tempeh, uttapam and dosa batter.

You can make yogurt directly in the stainless steel pot or in small mason jars. I typically use small glass jars because I feel the yogurt sets up better that way.

GENERAL PRESETS

All of these use the pressure cooking lid with the valve closed.

SOUP

- *Defaults to 30 minutes on high pressure.*
- *Pressing the adjust button changes the time (20 or 40 minutes).*

MEAT/STEW

- *Defaults to 35 minutes on high pressure.*
- *Pressing the adjust button changes the time (20 or 45 minutes).*

BEAN/CHILI

- *Defaults to 30 minutes on high pressure.*
- *Pressing the adjust button changes the time (25 or 40 minutes).*

POULTRY

- *Defaults to 15 minutes on high pressure.*
- *Pressing the adjust button changes the time (5 or 30 minutes).*

MULTIGRAIN

- *Defaults to 40 minutes on high pressure.*
- *Pressing the adjust button changes the time (45 or 60 minutes).*

Notice that on this setting, and only on the 60-minute cycle, the grain first gets a 45-minute warm water soaking time before the 60 minutes of pressure cooking time. This works great with oat groats and other grains that you typically soak before cooking. Try 1 cup (190 g) of unsoaked grain to 3 cups (708 ml) of water or broth and cook on this setting.

PORRIDGE OR CONGEE

- *Defaults to 20 minutes on high pressure.*
- *Pressing the adjust button changes the time (15 or 30 minutes).*

Special Diets

WHAT'S THE DIFFERENCE BETWEEN VEGAN AND PLANT-BASED?

If you've been vegan or plant-based for any length of time you may already know the answer to this question. If you're new to all this, it may seem confusing. The way I look at it is that vegan is an ethical choice to not consume any animal products. People who eat plant-based diets also don't eat any animal products, but they make their food choices based on how it will affect their health.

That's splitting it down the middle. There are lots of gray areas, and there are lots of points in between eating *only* for health and *only* for the animals. For example, there are people who eat healthy at home and splurge when eating out. Others may choose to eat healthy and care about animal welfare.

I don't see either path as being the right or wrong way to live. I believe you have to live the way that feels right for you. I create recipes and support for both sides, and I am glad you are on a journey to be your best self!

EATING A HEALTHY PLANT-BASED DIET

Isn't all vegan food healthy? In a word, no. There are cookies full of preservatives and other products that are accidentally vegan. They may taste good, but they aren't health promoting.

I have no judgements about your choices, but I just want to be clear that the recipes in this book can be adjusted for special diets such as Chef AJ's, Engine 2, Dr. McDougall, Dr. Campbell and more. Most of the recipes have options so you can customize any special diet.

LOW OR NO SALT

In most of the recipes I ask that you add salt to taste. The recipes that do call for a certain amount of salt usually need extra seasoning, or the salt needs to be added before the end. You can always substitute My Favorite Salt Substitute Blend recipe (page 32) or your favorite salt-free herb blend in savory recipes that call for salt. If it's a sweet recipe, just leave it out.

I also find that adding extra granulated garlic and onion powder can create that bite we usually get from salt.

NO ADDED OIL

If you are on a no-oil diet you will be able to make all of the recipes with a few adjustments.

While I offer the option to use a small amount of oil to sauté with, you can easily dry sauté or add a little water/vegetable broth in the Instant Pot. If you find your onions or garlic sticking, just add a bit more water or vegetable broth. If you are sautéing whole spices, such as cumin seeds or the like, sauté dry instead of water sautéing.

You can use applesauce or pumpkin puree in place of oil in baked goods. There's always a substitute you can use. You can even replace full-fat coconut milk with low-fat or use coconut extract and plain, unsweetened nondairy milk.

SOY-FREE

I've tried to provide substitutes or alternatives to soy products when used. You can use hemp tofu in any of the recipes in place of soy tofu or tempeh, and use almond milk, coconut milk or yogurt. You can substitute cauliflower, jackfruit and even chickpeas in many recipes that call for tofu or tempeh.

Note that the recipe in this book for tempeh (page 35) is actually soy-free, so if you can't have soy you've found the perfect reason to try making your own!

REFINED SUGAR-FREE

This means different things to different people. In most of the recipes, I call for you to use your sweetener of choice, to taste. This is so that you can accommodate your special diet. Date syrup and dates are widely accepted sweeteners, and I have a recipe for Instant Pot Date Syrup (page 46). Store-bought date syrup can be prohibitively expensive.

HOW DO YOU SWEETEN TO TASTE?

Because we're cooking vegan, you can actually taste a batter or mixture before it's cooked. So, what you'll do is exactly what I do when I'm developing a recipe. First, I add less sweetener than I think I'll need. You can always add more, but you can't take it back out. Mix it in well, taste and repeat until it's the way you want it.

Note that if you are making the Fresh Turmeric Ginger Tea Concentrate (page 155), you will actually want this to taste sweeter because it will be diluted. Or you can always add extra sweetener when you serve it.

Nutritional Information Disclaimer

Please note that the nutritional information is included in this book to give a ballpark idea on calories and the like. All of the recipes offer many options that could change the numbers drastically. If you have a medical condition that requires you to keep close track of those numbers, please enter the exact amount and ingredients you are using into the program that your doctor recommends.

The defaults used for the printed nutritional information are as follows:

- Unsweetened plain almond milk
- Salt substitute rather than salt
- No additional toppings
- Water sautéing option—the oil for oil sautéing is not included

staples

This is the most important chapter in my book. I love sharing how to make things that are so much less expensive than what you find in the store. You also get to control the ingredients that you put in, meaning that you can make them without salt, oil, refined sugar or something you are allergic to.

If you have an Instant Pot with a yogurt setting, try creating your own vegan yogurt, tempeh and other fermented recipes. I also have some special treats for you, including a homemade oil-free vegan cheese made out of beans (page 41), a dry bouillon (page 28) that you can keep in your cabinet and use at the drop of a hat, veggie dogs (page 37) made with real vegetables and even homemade date syrup (page 46).

Easy DIY Yogurt without Soy!

SOY-FREE. OIL-FREE.
REFINED SUGAR-FREE

Makes 8 servings

For this yogurt you'll want to use a fresh, unopened container of store-bought nondairy milk that contains pea protein. That way you know your milk is already pasteurized and you get to skip the step of boiling it and waiting for it to cool.

Why pea protein? The reason people use soy to make homemade yogurt is that it contains the protein needed to make the vegan yogurt thick naturally. Pea protein does the same thing. Look for nondairy milks in the refrigerated section that have 8 to 10 grams of protein, then check the ingredients.

Make in a 3-quart or 6-quart (3-L or 6-L) Instant Pot. Double and make in your 8-quart (8-L) Instant Pot.

1 (64-oz [1.9-L]) container nondairy milk that contains pea protein

2 packets vegan yogurt starter or 2 RenewLife Ultimate Flora Probiotic capsules

NOTE: I use Cultures for Health Vegan Yogurt Starter or contents of 2 RenewLife Ultimate Flora Probiotic capsules.

Whisk together the nondairy milk and starter in a very clean mixing bowl. Pour the mixture into small glass jars: I recommend using 4-ounce (114-ml) glass jelly jars. They can be easily sterilized and reused, and the yogurt thickens better in the smaller jars. Note: You do not need to use a rack.

Place the jars in your Instant Pot right on the bottom. Put on the lid. You don't have to close the valve, but if you do it could help the temperature stay more consistent.

Select the yogurt setting. The default time is 8 hours, but I find the yogurt gets firmer without an added thickener if you let it culture for 12 or more hours. Be aware that the yogurt will also become tangier the longer it cultures.

Store in the fridge for up to 10 days.

(continued)

Easy DIY Yogurt without Soy! (continued)

HOW TO MAKE GREEK YOGURT

Line a large strainer with a coffee filter. You can also use multiple layers of cheese cloth, but I think the coffee filter is easier to deal with and worth the investment if you want to make Greek yogurt often.

Set the strainer in a large bowl. Pour in the cultured yogurt. Place the bowl in your fridge and let it drain for 6 to 10 hours.

Use a spatula to scrape out every bit of the now-thick yogurt and store it in the fridge.

TROUBLESHOOTING

If your yogurt separates into whey—a yellowish liquid—and white thicker lumpy yogurt, don't panic. You can still make Greek yogurt by straining it. You can also do that even if it doesn't separate and you want a super thick yogurt.

If you strain it to troubleshoot you will probably need to blend it to make it smooth again. Place in the fridge and enjoy—I think this is better than plain yogurt.

If you use probiotic capsules, make sure to buy the ones in the refrigerated section of your health food store. These are going to work better.

You can use soy milk in this recipe. Just make sure it has as few ingredients as possible. You will probably find this in a 32-ounce (960-ml) container so you will need just half the amount of starter. Silk Protein works great. I love using their chocolate milk—it turns into a probiotic dessert!

PER SERVING: Calories 130.0, protein 10.0 g, total fat 8.0 g, carbohydrates 4.0 g, sodium 220.0 mg, fiber 0.5 g

No-Oil Vegan Corn Butter

This spread tastes amazingly like butter, and it has no added oil or nuts. The base is corn and you add some vegan lactic acid and powdered sunflower lecithin to make it taste like butter.

Make in a 3-quart or 6-quart (3-L or 6-L) Instant Pot. Double and make in your 8-quart (8-L) Instant Pot.

SOY-FREE, OIL-FREE, REFINED SUGAR-FREE

Makes about 1 cup (227 g)

PRESSURE COOKER INGREDIENTS

1½ cups (250 g) fresh or frozen corn kernels

1 cup (236 ml) water

BLENDER INGREDIENTS

1½ tbsp (11 g) tapioca starch

1 tsp salt or salt substitute

½ tsp vegan lactic acid (optional; adds a cultured taste)

½ tsp agar powder

½ tsp powdered sunflower lecithin (optional)

Add the corn and water to your Instant Pot and cook on high pressure for 5 minutes. Carefully release the pressure manually.

Add the corn mixture to a blender along with the tapioca starch, salt, vegan lactic acid (if using), agar powder and powdered sunflower lecithin (if using). Blend until smooth.

Add the mixture to a pan on the stove or to the Instant Pot liner. Whisk and sauté until the mixture begins to thicken and gets glossy, about 5 minutes.

Place in a resealable container and store in the fridge.

PER SERVING: Calories 16.0, protein 0.5 g, total fat 0.3 g, carbohydrates 3.4 g, sodium 2.3 mg, fiber 0.4 g

Instant Dry Vegetable Bouillon

SOY-FREE, OIL-FREE,
REFINED SUGAR-FREE

Makes about
10 tablespoons (54 g)

If you're like me, you've been caught with no homemade bouillon in the freezer and no store-bought in your pantry. This mix takes less than a minute to make and you can use 1 tablespoon (5 g) to replace a regular bouillon cube.

½ cup (48 g) nutritional yeast

1 tbsp (2 g) dried parsley

1 tsp dried thyme

1 tsp onion powder

1 tsp granulated garlic

½ tsp celery seeds

¼ tsp ground turmeric

¼ tsp paprika

Add the nutritional yeast, parsley, thyme, onion powder, granulated garlic, celery seeds, turmeric and paprika to a small food processor, spice grinder or small blender. Blend well. Store in a sealed airtight container for up to 6 months.

You can add other herbs if you'd like. I make mine salt-free, but you could add in salt and pepper, too.

Strawberry Chia Jam

Strawberry season is the best, but it's over far too soon. This is an easy way to preserve the taste of warm, sunny days all year long. Feel free to make large batches and freeze them for a winter treat.

Make in a 3-quart (3-L) Mini Instant Pot. Double and make in your 6-quart (6-L) Instant Pot.

SOY-FREE. OIL-FREE. REFINED SUGAR-FREE OPTION

Makes about 12 servings

2 cups (464 g) mashed strawberries, about 4 cups (576 g) before mashing

2 tsp (10 ml) balsamic vinegar

2 tbsp (22 g) white or black chia seeds

Sweetener of choice, to taste (optional; I used ½ cup [100 g] vegan sugar.)

Add the strawberries and balsamic vinegar to your Instant Pot liner.

Cook on manual/pressure cook for 3 minutes. Let the pressure release naturally. Turn off the Instant Pot.

Leave it chunky or use an immersion blender to make it smooth.

Add the chia seeds and turn the Instant Pot to sauté. Taste and add sweetener (if using) if the strawberries are not sweet enough on their own.

Leave the lid off and stir occasionally until the jam is as thick as you'd like it, about 3 to 5 minutes depending on how juicy the fruit is.

Store in the refrigerator or freeze it to enjoy all year long!

NOTE: If you are in a big hurry, let the pressure release naturally for at least 10 minutes then manually release the rest of the way. This is juicy so it could spray when the pressure is released, so be cautious.

I've also made this with peaches—you can really use any mashable fruit. Think berries, stone fruit and more!

PER SERVING: Calories 25.7, protein 0.8 g, total fat 0.9 g, carbohydrates 4.5 g, sodium 1.3 mg, fiber 1.9 g

My Favorite Salt Substitute Blend

SOY-FREE. OIL-FREE.
REFINED SUGAR-FREE

Makes about ½ cup
(about 54 g)

I know many of my blog readers are followers of various no-salt diets. It can be hard to find a salt substitute that you love, so I have a base recipe for you here. Please feel free to tweak depending on what you have on hand or just to suit your tastes.

¼ cup (24 g) nutritional yeast

2 tbsp (3 g) dried parsley

2 tbsp (12 g) tomato powder (can substitute carrot powder)

1 tbsp (8 g) granulated garlic

1½ tsp (2 g) dry ground lemon peel

1 tsp onion powder

1 tsp ground celery seed

1 tsp paprika

1 tsp dried basil

1 tsp dried thyme

1 tsp dried marjoram

¾ tsp mustard powder

Blend the nutritional yeast, parsley, tomato powder, granulated garlic, lemon peel, onion powder, celery seed, paprika, basil, thyme, marjoram and mustard powder together in a small food processor, small blender or spice grinder.

Store in an airtight container for up to 4 months.

Easy Homemade Tempeh

Making tempeh is easier than I thought it would be. The trick is to make sure you don't cook the beans too long and that they are completely dry before you add the vinegar and starter to them. Please note that fermentation can take longer than it's "supposed" to, but as long as you start to see the white mycelium continue to grow then it's working.

Make in a 6-quart or 8-quart (6-L or 8-L) Instant Pot.

PRESSURE COOKER INGREDIENTS

6 cups (1.4 L) water

1 lb (454 g) dry black-eyed peas

TEMPEH INGREDIENTS

1 tbsp (15 ml) white vinegar or pasteurized apple cider vinegar (Must NOT be raw or homemade!)

1 packet tempeh starter culture (I use Cultures for Health)

Add the water and black-eyed peas to your Instant Pot and cook on high pressure for 15 minutes. Release the pressure manually.

Drain and rinse the cooked beans. Strain the beans to make sure they are as dry as possible so the culture can do its job. I put two layers of paper towels or clean dish towels on two large cookie sheets. Then carefully spread the beans into as close to a single layer as you can. Cover with another layer of paper towels or a clean dish towel.

Let the beans sit for about 15 to 20 minutes. I carefully roll the layers up to get out the last of the moisture. You don't want to squish the beans.

Transfer the beans to a large, very clean bowl. Add in the white vinegar. Using a rice paddle or large wooden spoon, mix well without smashing the beans.

Add the tempeh starter culture and mix well; the culture needs to be as evenly distributed as possible.

Take two quart-sized (1-L) freezer bags and poke holes about 1 inch (2.5 cm) apart all over the bags in a grid format. You don't want the holes to be huge, so use a toothpick or metal skewer to make them.

Place half the bean mixture into each bag. You want to take up half the freezer bag and make it about 1 to 1½ inches (2.5 to 3.5 cm) thick.

Add the rack to your Instant Pot. Carefully, place the bags in without overlapping. In an 8-quart (8-L) Instant Pot you can lay both bags flat, but in a 6-quart (6-L) you will need to angle them a little.

(continued)

Easy Homemade Tempeh (continued)

Press the yogurt setting and set for 48 hours; make sure the lid is vented, or you can use the slow cooker lid if you have one. Note: You may need to repeat this step when you check on your tempeh.

Check the beans after 12 hours to see if you can see any of the white mycelium. You may only see specks at this point, but don't worry. Turn over the packets.

Check every 12 to 24 hours and flip. When the beans are solid and held together by the white spores, the tempeh is done. This can take 36 to 48 hours or more.

You can stop the culturing by placing the tempeh in the fridge. You can store it just like this for up to 10 days.

Not planning on eating it all in 10 days? You can freeze your tempeh, too. You just need to do one more step. Place each tempeh cake into boiling water for 30 seconds. Remove, dry and place in a freezer bag or freezer-safe container. It will freeze for up to 12 months.

WHY DOES THE VINEGAR NEED TO BE PASTEURIZED?

When we culture foods, we are encouraging good bacteria to grow. That means everything needs to be extra clean, or you could introduce bad bacteria. Pasteurization keeps those bad bacteria at bay. Unpasteurized vinegar is fine to use in cooking though.

ACK! MY TEMPEH HAS BLACK OR GRAY SPOTS!

It may look like your tempeh went bad when the white spores turn black or gray. This will most likely happen if you ferment too long, or it may just occur around the holes you poked in the bags. It's safe to eat as long as it's not moldy and it doesn't have a bad smell.

Veggie Dogs Made from Real Vegetables!

SOY-FREE, OIL-FREE, REFINED SUGAR-FREE

Makes 16 veggie dogs

I had been thinking about making a gluten-free veggie dog for a while. I wasn't sure if it was possible until I tasted Yeah Dawgs at the New England VegFest. They were amazing and inspired me to make this recipe. These are best with a second cook, so make the batch and then warm them up in the oven, air fryer or grill to serve.

Make in a 3-quart, 6-quart or 8-quart (3-L, 6-L or 8-L) Instant Pot.

1½ cups (355 ml) water

2 cups (300 g) chopped peeled potatoes

1½ cups (200 g) chopped peeled red beets, cut small

1 cup (130 g) chopped peeled carrot

1 cup (134 g) chopped peeled sweet potato

½ cup (102 g) brown rice flour, plus more for preparation

½ cup (58 g) teff flour, quinoa flour or soy flour

½ cup (50 g) oat flour

½ cup (60 g) tapioca starch or potato starch

¼ cup (24 g) nutritional yeast

2 tsp (12 g) salt or salt substitute

2 tsp (4 g) dried marjoram

1 tsp granulated garlic

1 tsp onion powder

1 tsp ground coriander

1 tsp paprika

Put 1½ cups (355 ml) of water in the bottom of your Instant Pot liner. Add the potatoes, beets, carrot and sweet potato into a steamer, then lower into your Instant Pot.

Cook on high pressure for 15 minutes. Release the pressure manually.

Place the cooked veggies in a very large mixing bowl. Mash well using a potato masher. You will need to seek out the beets, they will never mash as much as the other veggies.

In a separate bowl, mix the brown rice flour, teff flour, oat flour, tapioca starch, nutritional yeast, salt, marjoram, granulated garlic, onion powder, coriander and paprika together. Then slowly add to the mashed vegetables, making sure to incorporate thoroughly before adding in the next bit.

The mixture should get thick and clay-like once you've added all of the dry mix. Prepare a large cutting board by sprinkling with extra brown rice flour. This will keep the dogs from sticking.

Divide the dough into 16 equal balls on a cutting board. To make this quick and easy, you can use a ⅓-cup (80-ml) measuring cup and fill it a little less than full.

(continued)

Veggie Dogs Made from Real Vegetables! (continued)

At this point I go ahead and cut 16 equal pieces of parchment paper and foil for the dogs. Shape each one into a hot dog shape making the cylinder as even as possible. Wrap first in parchment paper, twist on the ends, then wrap in a piece of foil.

I use a deep mesh basket to cook the veggie dogs, but a steamer will work too. Make sure to angle them so that they do not smush each other. I usually only cook 8 at a time, so that they have some breathing room.

Add about 1 cup (236 ml) of water to your Instant Pot and lower in the basket with the dogs. Cook on high pressure for 35 minutes. Release the pressure manually.

Carefully remove the wrapped dogs and transfer to a cooling rack. Once cool enough to touch, unwrap and let "dry" on the rack for about 30 minutes.

I do not recommend eating these straight from the pressure cooker. Instead bake, grill or heat them in a pan or air fryer to get a better texture. Freeze what you won't be eating in the next week and bring them to cookouts or cook them for a quick no-effort meal another time.

PER SERVING: Calories 92.1, protein 2.6 g, total fat 0.6 g, carbohydrates 19.9 g, sodium 56.0 mg, fiber 2.7 g

Oil-Free Chickpea Sliceable Cheese

No nuts and no oil? Yes, it's true, here's a cheese for almost everyone. It gets a cheesy taste from vegan lactic acid in addition to the traditional nutritional yeast. This is a recipe that was started by Somer of VedgedOut.com then tweaked by Julie Hasson of juliehasson.com—and now it has been modified by me. It takes a village to make vegan cheese!

Be sure to try it on Chef AJ's Black Bean and Mushroom Chili (page 101) or Polenta Topped with Cannellini Bean Stew (page 130).

The downside is it does require you to invest in some ingredients. It will cost around $30 to get them, but you can make over a dozen batches.

SOY-FREE. OIL-FREE. REFINED SUGAR-FREE

Makes about 3 cups (340 g)

2 cups (475 ml) water

1½ cups (250 g) cooked chickpeas

2 tbsp (12 g) nutritional yeast

2 tsp (11 g) sea salt

1½ tsp (8 ml) lactic acid

½ tsp granulated onion

½ tsp granulated garlic

3 tbsp (33 g) tapioca starch

2 tbsp (10 g) kappa carrageenan

In the jar of a strong blender, combine the water, chickpeas, nutritional yeast, salt, lactic acid, granulated onion and garlic. Blend well.

Add the tapioca starch and kappa carrageenan, and blend for 5 to 10 seconds until smooth.

Pour the mixture into a large saucepan or your Instant Pot on sauté. Bring to a simmer over medium heat, whisking continually. Continue cooking, whisking continuously, for about 7 to 9 minutes, until the mixture has thickened nicely and is very glossy.

Pour the cheese into a container that can hold a minimum of 2 cups (475 ml) in volume. I like small loaf pans or glass bowls.

If properly cooked, the cheese will start to set right away. Allow the cheese to set at room temperature for 30 minutes. Then cover and refrigerate the cheese to finish setting for 3 to 4 hours.

If the cheese doesn't set up properly that means you haven't cooked it long enough. If this happens to you, throw it back into the saucepan and cook for a few minutes more! It will remelt and then you can pour it back into the mold for it to solidify.

Remove the cheese from the mold and serve. Store leftovers in the fridge. The cheese should last 10 to 14 days in the fridge.

PER SERVING: Calories 52.4, protein 2.4 g, total fat 0.5 g, carbohydrates 10.3 g, sodium 108.0 mg, fiber 1.9 g

Homemade Elderberry Syrup

When it's cold and flu season, everyone runs out to buy some pricey elderberry syrup. It's less expensive to make your own and you'll know exactly what went in it. You can make a double batch and freeze some, so you always have it on hand.

Make in a 3-quart, 6-quart or 8-quart (3-L, 6-L or 8-L) Instant Pot.

SOY-FREE. OIL-FREE. REFINED SUGAR-FREE OPTION

Makes about 2 cups (475 ml)

2 cups (475 ml) water

½ cup (73 g) dried elderberries

2 tbsp (6 g) chopped and peeled fresh ginger

2 tbsp (30 ml) lemon juice

1 whole cinnamon stick

1 tsp lemon zest

½ cup (118 ml) liquid sweetener, such as maple syrup, agave nectar or date syrup

Add the water, elderberries, ginger, lemon juice, cinnamon stick and lemon zest to your Instant Pot.

Cook on high pressure for 15 minutes and let the pressure release naturally. Use a potato masher to smash the berries.

Use a fine-mesh strainer to strain out the berries and spices. Add the sweetener and mix well. Store in the fridge for up to 3 months.

Take 1 to 2 teaspoons (5 to 10 ml) daily during cold and flu season, or when you are feeling under the weather.

Look for dried elderberries in the bulk spice section of your local natural food store or co-op. But don't forget that you can order them on Amazon from the comfort of your own living room.

Rainbow Vegetable Rice

SOY-FREE. OIL-FREE.
REFINED SUGAR-FREE

Makes about 10 servings

What if you could have something waiting in your freezer that would make dinner complete? Better yet, this rice made solely of minced veggies is good for you, too! I won't lie, it is labor intensive. Make it on a day you are not in a rush. I make a batch of this once a month and freeze 2 servings per freezer bag.

Add it under a stew such as Nancie's Green Curry Sweet Potatoes with Shiitake Mushrooms (page 113), make it a side for the Creole White Bean and Soy Curl Stew (page 87) or just pretty up a soup with a small scoop per bowl at the last minute.

This recipe requires a food processor, or you can hand grate if you have no other choice.

8 medium (624 g) carrots, peeled

1 small (265 g) head cauliflower, cut into florets

4 small (560 g) broccoli bunches with stems, cut into florets

1 small (794 g) red cabbage, outer leaves removed

You need two mixing bowls, one large and one extra-large that can hold 20 cups (4.7 L). You can use a large soup pot if you need to. We are making a giant batch of this so we only make the mess once, but you can benefit from it all week and maybe even all month.

Set up the food processor with the small shred blade. Shred the carrots, then transfer them to the smaller bowl. Change to the s-blade, then put the shredded carrots in and pulse until the shreds start to look like rice. Once ready, scrape them into the largest bowl.

Repeat with the cauliflower, broccoli and cabbage. Once they are all in the large bowl, mix the veggies together until combined thoroughly.

Leave out what you will use in the next 3 to 4 days. Freeze the rest in freezer bags or freezer-safe containers in the portion size that will feed you or your family for one meal. I freeze in 4-cup (960-ml) containers for the two of us. Go by what works best for you.

To cook on the stovetop, sauté in a large pan until just hot, about 3 minutes.

To cook in the Instant Pot, put 1½ cups (355 ml) of water in your Instant Pot. Add the amount of vegetable rice you will be cooking to a Pyrex or stainless container. You do not need to cover this container. Put the container on a rack in your Instant Pot and cook for 0 minutes and release the pressure as soon as the pot beeps that it's finished cooking.

PER SERVING: Calories 56.1, protein 4.5 g, total fat 0.5 g, carbohydrates 11.5 g, sodium 61.3 mg, fiber 5.3 g

Instant Pot Date Syrup

If you are looking for a natural sweetener, dates are the first thing that comes up. You can just use date paste, but date syrup gives a less muddy and more sophisticated flavor. It's expensive to buy, but easy to make. Use in the Creamy Corn Cinnamon Drink (page 152), Rosewater Kheer (page 156) or any recipe that calls for a sweetener.

Make in a 3-quart or 6-quart (3-L or 6-L) Instant Pot.

SOY-FREE. OIL-FREE. REFINED SUGAR-FREE

Makes about 1 cup (236 ml)

2 cups (475 ml) water

2 cups (300 g) chopped dates

Add the water and dates to your Instant Pot. Cook on high pressure for 20 minutes.

Let the pressure release naturally. Place a strainer over a large bowl and pour the mixture in. Use a potato masher and carefully mash the liquid out of the date pieces.

Rinse out the stainless steel liner and add the liquid back into it. Place the liner in your electric pressure cooker. Turn to sauté on high and—without the lid on—let the date syrup reduce by half. This will take about 15 minutes.

Store in the fridge. It will last for about 2 weeks.

PER SERVING: Calories 36.6, protein 0.3 g, total fat 0.1 g, carbohydrates 9.7 g, sodium 0.3 mg, fiber 1.0 g

DIY Cajun Seasoning Blend

SOY-FREE, OIL-FREE,
REFINED SUGAR-FREE

Makes about
2½ tablespoons (about 15 g)

This recipe will keep you in spicy goodness for a while—and it's a salt-free blend, too. It's a bonus that you can make it as spicy or mild as you want! You'll use this blend in the Creole White Bean and Soy Curl Stew (page 87) and in the New Orleans–Style Red Beans with Dirty Brown Rice (page 126).

2 tsp (4 g) paprika

2 tsp (3 g) dried thyme

2 tsp (4 g) dried oregano or marjoram

1 tsp granulated garlic

½ tsp onion powder

½–1 tsp cayenne pepper (depending on heat preference)

¼ tsp ground black pepper

¼ tsp allspice

⅛ tsp cloves

Mix the paprika, thyme, oregano, granulated garlic, onion powder, cayenne pepper, black pepper, allspice and cloves well. Store in a lidded container. You can also use a spice grinder to make it more like store-bought and to distribute the spices more evenly.

DIY Poultry Seasoning

Some people think that this has poultry in it. Don't worry—it's just a spice blend that's usually used on poultry. We add it to vegan dishes that need a boost of flavor. To me this seasoning smells just like Thanksgiving. Try it in the Quick One-Pot Chickeny Rice (page 73).

SOY-FREE. OIL-FREE.
REFINED SUGAR-FREE

Makes scant
6 tablespoons (24 g)

2 tbsp (4 g) dried sage

2 tbsp (5 g) dried thyme

1 tbsp (6 g) dried marjoram

2 tsp (9 g) celery seed

Mix the sage, thyme, marjoram and celery seed together. Store in an airtight container for about 3 months.

Easy Jamaican Curry Powder

This is used in Jamaican Jackfruit with Curry (page 116) and is also created by Michelle Blackwood of healthiersteps.com. It has some of the same spices as a garam masala, but the end result has a more Caribbean flare.

SOY-FREE, OIL-FREE, REFINED SUGAR-FREE

Makes scant
6 tablespoons (32 g)

2 tbsp (14 g) ground turmeric

2 tbsp (10 g) ground coriander

1 tbsp (7 g) ground cumin

1 tsp ground cardamom

½ tsp ground ginger

¼ tsp cayenne pepper, or to taste

Combine the turmeric, coriander, cumin, cardamom, ginger and cayenne pepper in a bowl. Store in an airtight container for about 3 months.

soups

I don't know about you, but I can't get enough soup. It's my go-to food in the winter, and I want it every day. If I'm under the weather, it's a brothy soup with vegetables that gets me back on me feet and feeling human again. It's taken me years to get Cheryl used to soup being a meal—and it was definitely worth the effort.

Soup is also the perfect first dish to make in your Instant Pot. Cleanup is easy because you sauté and cook in the same pot. I also love that you're not tied to the stove throughout the whole cooking process. Don't forget that if it's not a creamy soup, you can keep the leftovers in the freezer for a fast meal another time.

Velvety Root Veggie Soup

I love those in-between seasons like spring and fall. Both are great times for root vegetables. This soup is creamy from the veggies and even silky if you add the optional cashews. The flavors of all the veggies blend into one of the best bites of soup you may ever have.

SOY-FREE.
OIL-FREE OPTION.
REFINED SUGAR-FREE

Makes 4 servings

Make in a 3-quart, 6-quart or 8-quart (3-L, 6-L or 8-L) Instant Pot.

SAUTÉ INGREDIENTS

1 tbsp (15 ml) oil (or water sauté to make oil-free)

½ cup (75 g) minced onion

½ tsp minced garlic

PRESSURE COOKER INGREDIENTS

3 cups (708 ml) water

2 cups (300 g) chopped peeled potatoes

2 cups (220 g) chopped peeled apple

1 cup (130 g) chopped carrot

1 cup (150 g) chopped peeled rutabaga or peeled turnips

1 cup (150 g) chopped peeled butternut squash or peeled sweet potato

¼ cup (24 g) nutritional yeast

2 tbsp (19 g) cashews (optional)

1 tsp dried thyme

BEFORE SERVING

1–2 tsp (5–10 ml) balsamic vinegar, to taste

Salt and pepper, to taste

Turn your Instant Pot to sauté. Add the oil and sauté the onions until translucent, about 3 to 5 minutes. Add the garlic and sauté for 1 to 2 minutes.

Turn the sauté off, add the water, potatoes, apple, carrots, rutabaga, butternut squash, nutritional yeast, cashews (if using) and thyme.

Set the Instant Pot to manual/pressure cook and cook on high pressure for 15 minutes. Let the pressure release naturally for 15 minutes. This helps keep splattering to a minimum.

Use either a blender or an immersion blender to puree all the ingredients.

Add the balsamic vinegar, salt and pepper, to taste.

PER SERVING: Calories 195.8, protein 6.4 g, total fat 2.3 g, carbohydrates 42.1 g, sodium 53.4 mg, fiber 7.7 g

Easy Corn Chowder

I love corn soup recipes any time of the year, but corn chowder holds a special place in my heart when the weather gets chilly. Instead of making a traditional roux to thicken it, we just use an immersion blender to puree some of the soup.

Make in a 3-quart (3-L) Instant Pot. Double for a 6-quart (6-L) or triple for an 8-quart (8-L) Instant Pot.

SOY-FREE.
OIL-FREE OPTION.
REFINED SUGAR-FREE

Makes 4 servings

SAUTÉ INGREDIENTS

1 tbsp (15 ml) oil (or water sauté to make oil-free)

½ cup (75 g) minced onion

1 tsp minced garlic

PRESSURE COOKER INGREDIENTS

3 cups (708 ml) water

1 vegan bouillon cube or 1 tbsp (5 g) dry bouillon (page 28)

3 cups (450 g) chopped potatoes

3 cups (500 g) fresh or frozen corn kernels

1 cup (130 g) finely chopped or cubed carrot

1 tsp dried thyme

½ tsp dried marjoram

½ tsp liquid smoke or smoked paprika, or to taste

FOR SERVING

1 cup (236 ml) unsweetened nondairy milk

Salt and pepper, to taste

Turn your Instant Pot to sauté. Add the oil and sauté the onions until translucent, about 3 to 5 minutes. Add the garlic and sauté for 1 to 2 minutes.

Turn the sauté off, and add the water, bouillon, potatoes, corn, carrot, thyme, marjoram and liquid smoke.

Set the Instant Pot to manual/pressure cook and cook on high pressure for 10 minutes. Let the pressure release naturally for 10 minutes. This helps keep splattering to a minimum.

Remove the lid and add in the nondairy milk. Either use a blender or an immersion blender to just thicken the soup—don't puree all the way. You could also just puree a cup or two (236 or 475 ml) of the soup in a blender.

Mix well. Add salt and pepper, to taste.

PER SERVING: Calories 233.7, protein 7.2 g, total fat 1.9 g, carbohydrates 53.2 g, sodium 112.6 mg, fiber 7.5 g

Creamy Broccoli Soup

I remember back in my teen years being so proud of myself for eating that "healthy" cream of broccoli soup. Of course, then I had no idea it was filled with fat and salt and probably had very little broccoli in it at all. My version has lots more broccoli, is thickened with oats and cashews and cooks in just 1 minute. This is a great winter meal, a starter for a dinner party or a quick lunch.

Make in a 3-quart or 6-quart (3-L or 6-L) Instant Pot. Double and make in your 8-quart (8-L) Instant Pot.

SOY-FREE. OIL-FREE. REFINED SUGAR-FREE

Makes 6 servings

PRESSURE COOKER INGREDIENTS

4 cups (365 g) broccoli florets with stems peeled and chopped very small

3 cups (708 ml) water

¼ cup (23 g) gluten-free rolled oats

2 tbsp (19 g) raw cashews (leave out to make nut-free)

1 vegan bouillon cube or 1 tbsp (5 g) dry bouillon (page 28)

½ tsp minced garlic

½ tsp dried thyme

¼ tsp black pepper

¼ tsp ground nutmeg

Salt or salt substitute, to taste

TOPPINGS (OPTIONAL)

Steamed broccoli florets

Vegan shredded cheese

Dollop of plain vegan yogurt

Fresh green onions

Fresh grated nutmeg

Add the broccoli, water, oats, cashews, bouillon, garlic, thyme, black pepper and nutmeg to your Instant Pot. Cook on high pressure for 1 minute. Manually release the pressure.

Blend until smooth with an immersion blender. Taste and adjust any seasonings as needed. Season with salt or salt substitute. Serve with your favorite toppings.

Try this creamy soup with all your favorite veggies. Delicate veggies such as broccoli, summer squash and asparagus can cook in 1 minute. Try 10 minutes for potatoes, carrots, celery, sweet potatoes or winter squash.

It's best to not use a timer on this soup. If the oats sit in the water before cooking, they will become slimy.

Serve as is or fancy it up with one or more of the optional toppings.

PER SERVING: Calories 50.8, protein 1.7 g, total fat 1.5 g, carbohydrates 6.0 g, sodium 2.0 g, fiber 47.7 g

French-Style Mushroom Onion Soup

This brothy soup is rich with mushrooms and onions. The mushrooms give the broth a beefy flavor which soaks up in the gluten-free toast for an amazing meal. Some testers used mushroom broth to make it richer.

Make in a 3-quart (3-L) Instant Pot. Double for a 6-quart (6-L) or triple for an 8-quart (8-L) Instant Pot.

SOY-FREE.
OIL-FREE OPTION.
REFINED SUGAR-FREE

Makes 8 appetizer portions or 4 dinner portions

SAUTÉ INGREDIENTS

2 tbsp (30 ml) olive oil or vegan butter (or ¼ cup [59 ml] water to make oil-free)

2 cups (300 g) thinly sliced onions

8 oz (227 g) minced button or cremini mushrooms

½ tsp minced garlic

PRESSURE COOKER INGREDIENTS

3 cups (708 ml) water (or mushroom broth to make it richer)

1 bay leaf

1 tsp balsamic vinegar

½ tsp dried thyme or 4 small sprigs of fresh thyme

Salt and pepper, to taste

FOR SERVING (OPTIONAL, BUT RECOMMENDED)

Gluten-free and vegan bread, to toast

Vegan cheese, for melting

Turn on the sauté setting to low. Add the oil and cook the onions until translucent, about 8 minutes. Add the mushrooms and garlic. Sauté for 5 minutes, or until the mushrooms begin to release their liquid.

Turn the sauté off. Add the water, bay leaf, balsamic vinegar and thyme to your Instant Pot.

Cook on high pressure for 15 minutes. Let the pressure release naturally for 10 minutes, then release the pressure the rest of the way manually.

Before serving, remove the bay leaf. Add salt and pepper, to taste.

To make a more traditional French onion soup: Pour a serving of the soup in an oven-safe single-serving bowl. Toast your bread and place on top of the soup. Then melt your favorite vegan cheese on top in the oven. For the photo, I topped with a piece of toast and melted some vegan cheese with unsweetened nondairy milk to make my "melted" cheese.

PER SERVING: Calories 39.8, protein 1.4 g, total fat 0.5 g, carbohydrates 7.9 g, sodium 11.6 mg, fiber 1.7 g

Amy's Creamy Wild Rice Soup

My friend Amy Katz created this rich and creamy soup. It's easy to make and will warm you up on a cold winter night. Serve with a kale salad and some gluten-free crackers. I love that it includes wild rice!

SOY-FREE. OIL-FREE.
REFINED SUGAR-FREE

Makes 6 servings

Make in a 3-quart or 6-quart (3-L or 6-L) Instant Pot. Double and make in your 8-quart (8-L) Instant Pot.

SAUTÉ INGREDIENTS

2 tbsp (30 ml) water

1 cup (150 g) diced onion

2 cloves garlic, minced

1 cup (130 g) diced carrot

1 cup (100 g) diced celery

PRESSURE COOKER INGREDIENTS

1 cup (200 g) dried chickpeas, soaked overnight, drained and rinsed

1 cup (160 g) wild rice

1 bay leaf

1 tsp dried thyme

5 cups (1.2 L) vegetable broth or water

BEFORE SERVING

½ cup (75 g) raw cashews (soaked for 30 minutes in hot water if you don't have a high-speed blender)

½ cup (118 ml) water

Salt and pepper, to taste

Turn on the sauté setting and add the water. Add the onions and cook until translucent, 3 to 5 minutes. Add the garlic and sauté for 1 minute.

Add the carrots and celery and a few more splashes of water, as necessary, if the pot is dry. Sauté for a few minutes, until the vegetables are softened.

Add the soaked chickpeas, wild rice, bay leaf, thyme and vegetable broth. Stir to combine. Close the lid and cook on high pressure for 25 minutes.

While the soup is cooking, blend the cashews and water until very smooth in your blender. Set aside.

Release the pressure naturally. This time can vary, so if you're in a hurry you can let it release naturally for 10 minutes, then manually release the rest of the pressure.

Remove the lid once the pressure has released. Add the cashew mixture and stir well. Remove the bay leaf. Add salt and pepper, to taste. Adjust any seasonings as needed.

Make nut-free by using ¾ cup (180 ml) of nondairy unsweetened milk or creamer in place of the cashew cream.

PER SERVING: Calories 98.8, protein 3.8 g, total fat 0.7 g, carbohydrates 20.3 g, sodium 153.5 mg, fiber 3.7 g

Tortilla Soup with Jackfruit

I just love tortilla soup, and it's hard to find a good vegan version when you're out. Making a batch of this is a perfect excuse to stay in and save some money. You can make it as spicy as you want. After all, it's your kitchen.

This soup is easy to make with pantry ingredients. If you don't have a poblano, you can use green chilies. You could also substitute reconstituted soy curls, crumbled tempeh, tofu cubes or chickpeas for the jackfruit if you prefer.

Make in a 3-quart or 6-quart (3-L or 6-L) Instant Pot. Double and make in your 8-quart (8-L) Instant Pot.

SOY-FREE. OIL-FREE. REFINED SUGAR-FREE OPTION

Makes 4 servings

1 medium-size (150 g) onion, minced

2 cloves garlic, minced

1 poblano pepper, chopped (or 1 tbsp [15 g] green chilies)

4 cups (944 ml) vegetable broth (or water with a vegan bouillon cube)

1 (28-oz [794-g]) can crushed tomatoes

1 (10-oz [283-g]) jackfruit, drained and shredded by hand (or 1 [15-oz or 425-g] can chickpeas, drained and rinsed)

3 tbsp (50 g) tomato paste

1 tsp ground cumin

½ tsp chili powder

1 tsp maple syrup or sweetener of choice, or to taste

2 tbsp (12 g) nutritional yeast

Juice of ½ lime

Salt and pepper, to taste

FOR SERVING

Gluten-free tortilla chips, slightly crushed

½ avocado, peeled, pitted and chopped, then tossed with lime juice and chili powder

Cashew cream or vegan sour cream

1 tbsp (1 g) chopped fresh cilantro (optional)

Turn your Instant Pot to sauté. Dry or water sauté the onions until translucent, 3 to 5 minutes. Add the garlic and poblano, and sauté for 1 to 2 minutes. Turn sauté off.

Add the vegetable broth, tomatoes, jackfruit, tomato paste, cumin, chili powder and sweetener. Turn the Instant Pot to manual/pressure cook and cook on high pressure for 5 minutes.

Let the pressure release naturally, or let it release for at least 10 minutes and manually release the rest of the way.

Add the nutritional yeast, lime juice, salt and pepper. Top bowls of hot soup with crisp tortilla pieces, avocado, cashew cream and chopped cilantro (if using).

PER SERVING: Calories 391.3, protein 35.1 g, total fat 1.0 g, carbohydrates 114.0 g, sodium 565.8 mg, fiber 66.0 g

casseroles and pasta

The Instant Pot is wonderful for one-pot meals. Chickpeas and Dumplings (page 70), Quick One-Pot Chickeny Rice (page 73) and The Easiest Vegan Mac and Cheese (page 74) all remind me of childhood meals—but they are much better for me than the originals.

You can even make pasta dishes in your Instant Pot. The Creamy Mushroom Fettuccine (page 81) gets part of its creamy texture from the starch that comes from cooking the pasta in the Instant Pot with no draining. Don't forget that some gluten-free pastas hold up better than others. For traditional pastas, I recommend a corn-and-rice mixture or a quinoa rice. Some of the ones that have more whole grains often disintegrate while cooking.

Chickpeas and Dumplings

Being Southern I grew up on chicken and dumplings. In the South, our dumplings are more like thick noodle pieces and not the biscuit dumpling that you find in the Midwest. I like to switch out the chickpeas for other proteins that I have on hand, such as tofu or soy curls, or even extra vegetables.

SOY-FREE OPTION.
OIL-FREE OPTION.
REFINED SUGAR-FREE

Makes 6 servings

Make in a 6-quart (6-L) Instant Pot. Cut the recipe in half to make in a 3-quart (3-L) Instant Pot. Double and make in your 8-quart (8-L) Instant Pot.

1 tbsp (15 ml) oil (or water sauté to make oil-free)

1 cup (150 g) minced onion

1 cup (100 g) chopped celery

1 cup (130 g) diced carrot

1 tsp minced garlic

3 cups (708 ml) water

2 (15.5-oz [439-g]) cans chickpeas, drained and rinsed (or 3 cups [500 g] cooked chickpeas)

¼ cup + 2 tbsp (36 g) nutritional yeast, divided

1½ tsp (3 g) dried marjoram

1½ tsp (2 g) dried thyme

1½ tsp (9 g) salt, divided

¼ tsp black pepper

1 cup (120 g) gluten-free baking blend, plus more for sprinkling

¼ tsp baking powder

3 tbsp (45 g) coconut oil

½ cup (118 ml) nondairy milk mixed with 1 tsp apple cider vinegar

1 cup (135 g) frozen green peas

Turn your Instant Pot to sauté. Add the oil and cook the onions until translucent, 3 to 5 minutes. Add the celery, carrots and garlic. Cook for about 5 minutes.

Turn the sauté off, then add the water, chickpeas, ¼ cup (24 g) of nutritional yeast, marjoram, thyme, 1 teaspoon of salt and pepper to your Instant Pot. Cook on high pressure for 15 minutes.

Make the dumplings while the stew is cooking. Mix the baking blend with ½ teaspoon salt and baking powder in a mixing bowl. Using a pastry cutter or two knives, cut in the coconut oil until the mixture resembles a coarse cornmeal. Add the milk and mix well.

Sprinkle extra baking blend on a large cutting board and roll the dough out about ¼ inch (6 mm) thick. Cut into 1 x 2–inch (2.5 x 5–cm) rectangles.

Manually release the pressure on the stew and place the dumplings on top. Carefully mix without breaking up the dumplings.

Cook on high pressure for 7 minutes. Manually release the pressure. Stir in the remaining nutritional yeast and frozen peas. Press cancel, then sauté on low until the green peas are ready to eat. You can add more water as needed.

Make this plant-based by using a salt substitute and replacing the dumplings with potato chunks. Just add 2 cups (300 g) of chopped potatoes in with the stew. Skip the dumpling instructions, but still add the peas at the end!

PER SERVING: Calories 291.7, protein 9.4 g, total fat 9.9 g, carbohydrates 43.1 g, sodium 56.0 mg, fiber 8.4 g

Quick One-Pot Chickeny Rice

This is one of my signature versatile recipes that has all the options! I make it with whatever I have on hand. You can use a commercial gluten-free chicken substitute, such as Gardein Chick'n Scallopini or reconstituted soy curls. Or you can use chickpeas, tempeh, tofu or use additional carrots and potatoes instead.

SOY-FREE OPTION.
OIL-FREE OPTION.
REFINED SUGAR-FREE

Makes 4 servings

Make in a 3-quart or 6-quart (3-L or 6-L) Instant Pot. Double and make in your 8-quart (8-L) Instant Pot.

PRESSURE COOKER INGREDIENTS

2 cups (475 ml) water

2 vegan bouillon cubes or 2 tbsp (10 g) dry bouillon (page 28)

1 tsp DIY Poultry Seasoning (page 50)

2 cups (weight will vary) frozen mix veggies (corn, carrots and green beans)

1½ cups (280 g) white jasmine or basmati rice

1 (10-oz [285-g]) package Gardein Chick'n Scallopini, chopped (or make it oil-free with 2 cups [about 330 g] cooked chickpeas, hydrated soy curls, tempeh crumbles or tofu chunks)

BEFORE SERVING

2 tbsp (12 g) nutritional yeast, or to taste (I used ¼ cup [24 g])

Salt and pepper, to taste

In a measuring cup, mix the water with the bouillon and poultry seasoning. Layer the following in your Instant Pot: the veggies on the bottom, followed by the rice and the water mixture. Push the rice under the liquid. Top with the protein.

Cook on high pressure for 7 minutes and manually release the pressure.

Stir in the nutritional yeast, salt and pepper until it's just right for you.

Use this quick-cooking recipe as a base and try it a few different ways. Leave out the poultry seasoning and:

- Add in 1½ cups (258 g) of cooked black beans and 1 cup (260 g) of salsa, then top with vegan cheese and cilantro.

- Add in 1 tablespoon (6 g) of garam masala and serve with a side of vegan yogurt.

PER SERVING: Calories 408.3, protein 23.9 g, total fat 5.1 g, carbohydrates 67.4 g, sodium 576.7 mg, fiber 3.8 g

The Easiest Vegan Mac and Cheese

Some nights you need a quick dinner that doesn't take much effort to make. This one has the added bonus of being easy on your wallet, too. This mac and cheese is simple to make and uses pantry ingredients!

Make in a 3-quart or 6-quart (3-L or 6-L) Instant Pot.

SOY-FREE.
OIL-FREE OPTION

Makes 4 servings

PRESSURE COOKER INGREDIENTS

3 cups (708 ml) water

1 (8-oz [227-g]) package gluten-free macaroni made with corn and rice (Barilla or Walmart brand)

2 tsp (10 ml) olive oil or vegan butter (optional; leave out to make oil-free)

SAUCE INGREDIENTS

6 tbsp (36 g) nutritional yeast

¼ cup (59 ml) unsweetened nondairy milk

½ tsp granulated garlic

½ tsp smoked paprika

¼ tsp mustard powder

¼ tsp ground turmeric

Salt and pepper, to taste

Add the water, macaroni and oil (if using) to your Instant Pot liner. Set the Instant Pot to manual/pressure cook and cook on high pressure for 5 minutes. Carefully release the pressure manually.

Stir in the nutritional yeast, nondairy milk, granulated garlic, smoked paprika, mustard powder and turmeric. Add salt and pepper, to taste.

If the mixture has too much liquid, press the cancel button and then set the sauté to low. Cook until the mac and cheese reaches the desired texture, about 5 to 10 minutes.

PER SERVING: Calories 241.9, protein 8.6 g, total fat 1.7 g, carbohydrates 51.1 g, sodium 13.1 mg, fiber 3.6 g

Vegetable Pad Thai

This seems to be everyone's favorite Thai dish. It has lots of flavor, and it's slightly sweet which seems to lure picky eaters into trying it. The noodles will be a little sticky because we aren't rinsing them after cooking. If you hate sticky noodles, cook them separately on the stove and add them right before serving. Either way, it's a great way to eat Thai at home.

Make in a 3-quart or 6-quart (3-L or 6-L) Instant Pot. Double and make in your 8-quart (8-L) Instant Pot.

SOY-FREE OPTION,
OIL-FREE, REFINED
SUGAR-FREE OPTION

Makes 4 servings

SAUCE INGREDIENTS

¼ cup (59 ml) gluten-free tamari (or gluten-free soy sauce, Bragg Liquid Aminos or coconut aminos)

¼ cup (50 g) coconut sugar, brown sugar or sweetener of choice, or to taste

1 tbsp (7 g) fresh grated ginger

1½ tsp (4 g) minced garlic

2 tsp (10 ml) Sriracha, or to taste (plus more for serving)

PRESSURE COOKER INGREDIENTS

1½ cups (355 ml) water

1 (8-oz [227-g]) package brown rice pad Thai noodles

2 cups (300 g) julienned bell pepper

1 cup (125 g) julienned carrot

½ (4-oz [114-g]) package soy curls, reconstituted and drained, or 3 cups (500 g) cooked chickpeas, 3 cups (465 g) edamame or 3 cups (700 g) cubed super firm tofu (optional)

3 cups (275 g) broccoli florets

TOPPINGS (OPTIONAL)

2 cups (220 g) shredded or spiralized carrots

2 cups (200 g) fresh bean sprouts

1 cup (145 g) chopped peanuts

2 limes, quartered

Whisk together the tamari, coconut sugar, ginger, garlic and Sriracha. Add the sauce mixture and the water to your Instant Pot liner and mix them together. Layer the noodles in first and keep them as even as possible. Top with bell pepper and carrot. Add the protein (if using) and top with the broccoli florets.

Cook on high pressure for 2 minutes. Manually release the pressure. I like to remove the broccoli and/or tofu or other addition with tongs and put it on a plate so it doesn't continue cooking. If the broccoli is underdone, leave it in.

Add any removed veggies or tofu back to your Instant Pot and unstick the noodles where needed. Serve on a platter with toppings (if using) and extra Sriracha.

PER SERVING (EVERYTHING BUT THE OPTIONAL ADD-INS): Calories 314.2, protein 17.8 g, total fat 1.2 g, carbohydrates 68.5 g, sodium 1 g, fiber 7.2 g

Eggplant Tomato Pasta Sauce

Some nights call for a hearty pasta sauce that's easy to make and will impress your nonvegan guests. This is the sauce for you. You can use mushrooms or gluten-free vegan beefy crumbles to add bulk and flavor. Serve over your favorite pasta, rice or even toasted gluten-free bread.

SOY-FREE, OIL-FREE, REFINED SUGAR-FREE

Makes 8 servings

Make in a 3-quart or 6-quart (3-L or 6-L) Instant Pot. Double and make in your 8-quart (8-L) Instant Pot.

SAUTÉ INGREDIENTS

1 tbsp (15 ml) olive oil (or water sauté to make oil-free)

1 medium (150 g) onion, minced

1 tbsp (9 g) minced garlic

1 medium (120 g) green pepper, chopped

PRESSURE COOKER INGREDIENTS

2 (28-oz [794-g]) cans crushed tomatoes

2 cups (165 g) peeled and chopped eggplant

2 cups (220 g) gluten-free vegan beefy crumbles or minced mushrooms

½ cup (118 ml) water

1½ tbsp (7 g) dried basil

1 tbsp (5 g) dried oregano

1½ tsp (3 g) powdered rosemary

BEFORE SERVING

1 tbsp (15 ml) balsamic vinegar

Salt and pepper, to taste

Turn your Instant Pot to sauté. Add the oil and cook the onion until translucent, 3 to 5 minutes. Add the garlic and green pepper, and sauté for about 3 minutes.

Turn the sauté off, then add the tomatoes, eggplant, vegan beefy crumbles, water, basil, oregano and rosemary to your Instant Pot.

Cook on high pressure for 25 minutes. Let the pressure release naturally for 10 minutes, then release the pressure the rest of the way manually.

Add the balsamic vinegar, stir, then add salt and pepper, to taste.

If your electric pressure cooker doesn't get up to pressure or gives the burn message, it means that there wasn't enough liquid. Stop and add another ½ cup (118 ml) of water in a 6-quart (6-L) Instant Pot or 1 cup (236 ml) in an 8-quart (8-L). This can happen if the veggies you use are a little drier.

PER SERVING: Calories 60.5, protein 2.7 g, total fat 0.2 g, carbohydrates 14.0 g, sodium 304.8 mg, fiber 1.2 g

Creamy Mushroom Fettuccine

This is my go-to fancy pasta that requires very little effort. After a quick sauté, you dump the rest of the ingredients in—and you end up with a pasta dish you could get in a restaurant!

Make in a 6-quart (6-L) Instant Pot. Cut the recipe in half to make in a 3-quart (3-L) Instant Pot. Double and make in your 8-quart (8-L) Instant Pot.

SOY-FREE,
OIL-FREE OPTION,
REFINED SUGAR-FREE

Makes 4 large servings

SAUTÉ INGREDIENTS

1 tbsp (15 ml) olive oil (or water sauté to make oil-free)

½ cup (75 g) minced onion

1 tsp minced garlic

8 oz (227 g) chopped mushrooms (about 3 cups)

PRESSURE COOKER INGREDIENTS

6 tbsp (36 g) nutritional yeast

1 small sprig of fresh rosemary or ¼ tsp ground rosemary

4 cups (944 ml) water

1 (12-oz [340-g]) box gluten-free corn-and-rice fettuccine

BEFORE SERVING

½ cup (118 ml) unsweetened nondairy milk or creamer

Salt and pepper, to taste

Turn your Instant Pot to sauté. Add the oil and cook the onion until translucent, 3 to 5 minutes. Add the garlic and mushrooms. Sauté until the mushrooms are cooked down, 5 to 10 minutes.

Turn the sauté off, then stir the nutritional yeast and rosemary into the mushroom mixture. Spread the mixture evenly on the bottom of the pot. Pour in the water.

Snap the fettuccine in half and fan it over the mushroom mixture. Make sure the pasta is submersed. The fanning and the submersion will help the pasta not stick together as much.

Put the lid on and cook on high pressure for 10 minutes. Manually release the pressure carefully. Use a spoon to mix everything together and separate any pasta pieces that are sticking together.

Stir in the nondairy milk, and add salt and pepper, to taste. Adjust any seasonings as needed.

If the mixture is too watery, turn to sauté and cook off the extra liquid.

The corn-and-rice pasta is my go-to because it holds up so well. I've had some expensive gluten-free pasta all but dissolve in regular boiling water on the stove. You can experiment with pasta, but do it with caution and not on a dinner party night.

PER SERVING: Calories 347.6, protein 10.8 g, total fat 2.0 g, carbohydrates 77.0 g, sodium 27.2 mg, fiber 5.9 g

beans

Dried beans are one of the first reasons many people start to use an Instant Pot. Beans cook in half the time—and that gets you back more time in your day.

I know many of you prefer to soak your beans before you cook them. I've added in quick-soak instructions in case you want to make the recipe without waiting a day for your beans to soak the old-fashioned way. If you have soaked your beans, just ignore the quick-soak instructions.

If you want to cook dry beans without any kind of soaking, use at least twice as much water as called for and cook for about twice as long. This is a rule of thumb. You can find a general Bean Cooking Chart on page 167.

Also keep in mind that beans are always the variable: You can never really know how old the beans are unless you grow them yourself or buy them from Rancho Gordo. Rancho Gordo sells the beans as they pick them. Older beans can take more time to cook, so be prepared to let them cook a little longer.

Onion and Molasses Baked Beans

You can take these vegan baked beans to a cookout or enjoy a bowl in front of a fire in the winter. For a fun dinner, add some cut homemade veggie dogs (page 37). These beans are thick and rich—even nonvegans will ask for seconds.

SOY-FREE.
OIL-FREE OPTION.
REFINED SUGAR-FREE OPTION

Makes about 14 servings

Make in a 3-quart, 6-quart or 8-quart (3-L, 6-L or 8-L) Instant Pot.

QUICK-SOAK INGREDIENTS

1 lb (454 g) dry cranberry beans, pinto beans or navy beans

6 cups (1.4 L) water

SAUTÉ INGREDIENTS

1 tbsp (15 ml) oil (or water sauté to make oil-free)

1 cup (150 g) chopped onion

PRESSURE COOKER INGREDIENTS

4 cups (944 ml) water

2 cups (220 g) minced peeled apple

3 tbsp (45 ml) Dijon mustard

2 tbsp (30 ml) molasses

2 tsp (3 g) dried thyme

2 tsp (10 ml) liquid smoke

BEFORE SERVING

¼ cup (50 g) brown sugar or maple syrup (optional)

3 tbsp (45 ml) tomato paste

2 tbsp (30 ml) apple cider vinegar

Salt, to taste

Put the dry beans and water into your electric pressure cooker. Cook on high pressure for 8 minutes. Manually release the pressure. Drain the quick-soaked beans and rinse the beans and the inner liner.

On the sauté setting, heat the oil. Once hot, add the onion and cook until translucent, 3 to 5 minutes. Add the water, apple, mustard, molasses, thyme and liquid smoke to your Instant Pot along with the quick-soaked beans.

Cook on high pressure for 15 minutes. Carefully release the pressure manually. Try to mash one of the beans with a fork to see if it is soft. If not, put the lid back on and cook for 5 minutes.

Release the pressure manually. Stir in the brown sugar, tomato paste and vinegar. Add the salt, to taste.

If there's too much liquid left, you can always turn your Instant Pot to sauté and cook off any extra liquid.

PER SERVING: Calories 125.5, protein 7.8 g, total fat 0.1 g, carbohydrates 30.3 g, sodium 107.8 mg, fiber 9.1 g

Creole White Bean and Soy Curl Stew

SOY-FREE OPTION.
OIL-FREE OPTION

Makes 4 servings

I lived in New Orleans for twelve years, and I love a New Orleans–inspired recipe. In addition to the creamy beans that they're famous for, I've added some sun-dried tomatoes to punch up the flavor and some soy curls to make it heartier. I like to serve this with thick sliced toast with corn butter or over steamed brown rice.

Make in a 3-quart, 6-quart or 8-quart (3-L, 6-L or 8-L) Instant Pot.

PRE-SOAK INGREDIENTS

1 lb (454 g) white beans, such as Great Northern beans or cannellini beans

6 cups (1.4 L) water

SAUTÉ INGREDIENTS

1 tbsp (15 ml) oil (or water sauté to make oil-free)

1 cup (150 g) minced onion

1 tsp minced garlic

1 cup (150 g) minced red bell pepper

1 tbsp (6 g) DIY Cajun Seasoning Blend (page 49)

½ tsp ground celery seed

PROTEIN INGREDIENTS

2 cups (80 g) dried soy curls, broken into small pieces, reconstituted and drained (or 2 cups [466 g] cubed tofu, 2 cups [335 g] crumbled tempeh or 2 cups [330 g] cooked chickpeas)

2 tbsp (12 g) nutritional yeast

1 tsp dry bouillon (page 28; optional)

PRESSURE COOKER INGREDIENTS

4 cups (944 ml) water

1 vegan bouillon cube or 1 tbsp (5 g) dry bouillon (page 28)

¼ cup (14 g) minced sun-dried tomatoes

If you haven't soaked your beans overnight, add the beans and water to your Instant Pot. Cook on high for 8 minutes and manually release the pressure. Pour into a strainer and rinse the beans and the Instant Pot liner.

Turn the sauté setting on low. Add the oil and cook the onion until translucent, about 8 minutes. Add the garlic, bell pepper, Cajun seasoning and celery seed. Cook for about 5 minutes. Turn the sauté off.

Mix together the soy curls, nutritional yeast and bouillon (if using). Add this to the pressure cooker with the beans, water, bouillon cube and sun-dried tomatoes.

Cook on high pressure for 10 minutes. Manually release the pressure.

Make this soy-free by leaving out the soy curls. Easy peasy!

PER SERVING: Calories 430.0, protein 45.8 g, total fat 9.1 g, carbohydrates 87.2 g, sodium 156.7 mg, fiber 47.7 g

Mayocoba Refried Beans

SOY-FREE. OIL-FREE

Makes 8 servings

I love saving money by cooking dried beans—they're just so much less expensive than canned beans. It also opens up a world of new bean varieties. Mayocoba beans are sometimes known as canary beans, and you can find them at Hispanic markets as well as some national supermarkets. Who knew a little yellow bean could cook up so creamy? If you can't find mayocoba beans, just substitute pintos or black beans.

Make in a 3-quart or 6-quart (3-L or 6-L) Instant Pot. Double and make in your 8-quart (8-L) Instant Pot.

1 lb (454 g) dry mayocoba beans, soaked overnight (or use pinto or black beans)

2 cups (475 ml) water

1 tbsp (5 g) dried oregano, plus more to taste

2 tsp (3 g) granulated garlic, plus more to taste

1 tsp onion powder, plus more to taste

½ tsp jalapeño powder, plus more to taste

Salt, to taste

Drain the soaked beans. Add the beans, water, oregano, granulated garlic, onion powder and jalapeño powder to the liner of your Instant Pot and stir. Cook on high pressure for 15 minutes.

Carefully release the pressure manually. Try to mash one of the beans with a fork to see if it is soft. If not, put the lid back on and cook for 5 minutes.

Mash the beans with a potato masher or you can use an immersion blender to get them extra smooth. Taste, add salt and adjust the seasonings if you'd like them to be stronger. I like them mild because I serve them with salsa and other toppings.

If there's too much liquid left, you can turn your Instant Pot to sauté and cook off any extra liquid.

Can't find mayocoba beans where you live? You can order them on Amazon or just substitute with black or pinto beans.

PER SERVING: Calories 270.0, protein 18.0 g, total fat 2.3 g, carbohydrates 47.3 g, sodium 0.0 mg, fiber 20.3 g

Sonal's Red Lentil Dal with Mint and Garlic

SOY-FREE, OIL-FREE OPTION

Makes 4 servings

I love that my friend Sonal Gupta's red lentil dal is authentic and uses ingredients you can get at a regular grocery store. Once cooked, it's so creamy and light, making it perfect for a quick Indian meal on a weeknight.

Make in a 3-quart or 6-quart (3-L or 6-L) Instant Pot. Double and make in your 8-quart (8-L) Instant Pot.

SAUTÉ INGREDIENTS

½ tbsp (8 ml) mild oil (or dry sauté to make oil-free)

1 tsp cumin seeds

4 large cloves garlic, minced

1 tsp fresh ginger, minced

1 green chili, minced (optional)

1 tsp ground turmeric

½ tsp red chili powder or cayenne pepper (use less for less heat)

½ tsp garam masala

1 tsp dried mint (or 1 tbsp [6 g] finely chopped fresh mint)

PRESSURE COOKER INGREDIENTS

4 cups (944 ml) water

1 cup (200 g) red lentils, washed and drained

BEFORE SERVING

1½ tsp (9 g) salt, or to taste

GARNISHES (OPTIONAL)

Sprinkle of dry mint leaves or a few fresh mint leaves

Dash of lemon juice

Turn your Instant Pot sauté setting on low. Add the oil and cook the cumin seeds for a few seconds. Add the garlic, ginger and green chili (if using). Sauté until the garlic becomes golden in color. Add the turmeric, red chili powder, garam masala and mint. Stir well.

Add the water and lentils. Cook on high pressure for 5 minutes. Let the pressure release naturally. Add the salt.

Garnish with mint leaves and/or a sprinkle of lemon juice (if using).

(continued)

Sonal's Red Lentil Dal with Mint and Garlic (continued)

Sonal has added an optional tempering recipe for the spice topping. In many Indian dishes, spices are sautéed or tempered with oil. This gives the dish a flavor burst when drizzled on top.

½ tbsp (8 ml) cooking oil

1 tsp cumin seeds

1 large clove garlic, sliced or chopped thin

¼–½ tsp cayenne pepper or red chili powder

Heat the oil in a frying pan. Once the oil is hot, lower the heat to medium. Add the cumin seeds and garlic. Sauté until the garlic turns golden, then add the cayenne pepper and immediately turn off the heat. Stir well. Now add this mixture to the dal.

PER SERVING: Calories 154.9, protein 11.2 g, total fat 0.0 g, carbohydrates 28.1 g, sodium 0.6 mg, fiber 7.1 g

Greek-Spiced Lentil Stew

This is a delicately flavored stew that's a great way to introduce eggplant to your family's diet. This lentil stew is comfort in a bowl, especially when served over mashed potatoes. I love that it freezes well, and I keep a serving hidden away for nights when I'm too tired to cook from scratch.

Make in a 3-quart or 6-quart (3-L or 6-L) Instant Pot. Double and make in your 8-quart (8-L) Instant Pot.

SOY-FREE.
OIL-FREE OPTION.
REFINED SUGAR-FREE

Makes 6 servings

SAUTÉ INGREDIENTS

1 tbsp (15 ml) oil (or water sauté to make oil-free)

1 cup (150 g) minced onion

1 tsp minced garlic

PRESSURE COOKER INGREDIENTS

4 cups (944 ml) water

2 cups (165 g) chopped eggplant

2 cups (400 g) brown lentils

1 cup (130 g) chopped carrot

1 bay leaf

1 tbsp (5 g) dried oregano

1½ tsp (3 g) paprika

1½ tsp (3 g) ground cinnamon

1 tsp ground coriander

2 pinches of ground cloves

BEFORE SERVING

2 tbsp (12 g) nutritional yeast

Juice of ½ small lemon

Salt and pepper, to taste (or use salt substitute)

FOR SERVING (OPTIONAL)

Cooked brown rice or mashed potatoes

Turn your Instant Pot to sauté. Add the oil and cook the onion until translucent, 3 to 5 minutes. Add the garlic and sauté for 1 minute.

Turn the sauté off, then add the water, eggplant, lentils, carrot, bay leaf, oregano, paprika, cinnamon, coriander and cloves to your Instant Pot. Stir well. Cook on high pressure for 12 minutes and manually release the pressure.

Stir in the nutritional yeast and lemon juice. Remove the bay leaf, then add salt and pepper, to taste. Serve plain in a bowl, or enjoy over steamed rice or mashed potatoes (next page).

PER SERVING: Calories 103.2, protein 6.8 g, total fat 0.4 g, carbohydrates 19.4 g, sodium 17.7 mg, fiber 7.0 g

(continued)

EASY IP MASHED POTATOES

Make in a 3-quart, 6-quart or 8-quart (3-L, 6-L or 8-L) Instant Pot.

You won't believe how easy it is to make mashed potatoes in your Instant Pot. Cut peeled potatoes in chunks and they'll be ready in a flash.

Makes about 6 servings

4 large russet potatoes, peeled and cut into chunks

Water, to cover

Unsweetened nondairy milk

Olive oil or vegan butter, to taste (optional)

Add the potatoes and water to your electric pressure cooker. Cook on high pressure for 10 minutes. Carefully release the pressure manually.

Pour the contents of the Instant Pot into a colander over the sink to drain the water. Add the drained potatoes to a metal mixing bowl or pot. Mash and add small amount of unsweetened nondairy milk until it's the texture you want.

If you cook with oil, add some olive oil or vegan butter to make them extra decadent.

PER SERVING: Calories 98.0, protein 2.4 g, total fat 0.1 g, carbohydrates 22.3 g, sodium 22.6 mg, fiber 3.4 g

Anu's Moong Dal Khichdi (Indian Lentil and Rice Porridge)

SOY-FREE,
OIL-FREE OPTION

Makes 4 servings

Moong dal khichdi is perfect when you have an upset stomach and need to eat something mild and soothing. I think of it as Indian congee because both contain rice cooked into a thick and comforting stew. This is my friend Anu's version, and it's my go-to when I'm feeling under the weather.

Make in a 3-quart or 6-quart (3-L or 6-L) Instant Pot. Double and make in your 8-quart (8-L) Instant Pot.

SAUTÉ INGREDIENTS

1 tbsp (15 ml) mild oil (or dry sauté to make oil-free)

1 tsp cumin seeds

PRESSURE COOKER INGREDIENTS

¾ cup (150 g) rice, rinsed and drained

¾ cup (150 g) moong dal, rinsed and drained

½ tsp ground turmeric

Pinch of asafoetida (optional; always check for gluten-free on the label)

4 cups (944 ml) water

Salt, to taste

Add the oil to the Instant Pot liner and press sauté. Add the cumin seeds. When they start to splutter, add the rice, moong dal, turmeric and asafoetida (if using). Add the water and mix well.

Cover with the Instant Pot lid and lock it. Press the warm/cancel button and then select pressure cook. Adjust the time to 10 minutes and pressure selection to high, or you can select the porridge setting.

Let the pressure release naturally. Add salt, to taste.

PER SERVING: Calories 297.0, protein 12.0 g, total fat 4.0 g, carbohydrates 51.0 g, sodium 14.0 mg, fiber 4.0 g

Veggie Hunter's Lentil Quinoa Stew

This is a hearty stew, and it's full of umami flavor from the mushrooms and lentils. The herbs brighten it up a little and the quinoa adds a ton of protein. The Romanesco is a fun seasonal addition, but cauliflower works fine when there's none to be found.

Make in a 3-quart or 6-quart (3-L or 6-L) Instant Pot. Double and make in your 8-quart (8-L) Instant Pot.

SOY-FREE.
OIL-FREE OPTION.
REFINED SUGAR-FREE

Makes 4 servings

SAUTÉ INGREDIENTS

1 tbsp (15 ml) oil (or water sauté to make oil-free)

1 medium (150 g) onion, minced

½ tsp minced garlic

2 cups (150 g) minced mushrooms

2 tbsp (15 g) minced celery or 1 tsp celery seeds

1 cup (180 g) tri-color quinoa, or any color

PRESSURE COOKER INGREDIENTS

2½ cups (590 ml) water

1 cup (140 g) chopped golden beets

¾ cup (150 g) black beluga lentils (can substitute French lentils)

½ cup (65 g) chopped carrot

2 small bay leaves

1½ tsp (3 g) dried marjoram

1 tsp dried thyme

½ tsp dried basil

2 cups (680 g) Romanesco or cauliflower florets

Turn your Instant Pot to sauté. Add the oil and cook the onion until translucent, 3 to 5 minutes. Add the garlic and mushrooms. Sauté until the mushrooms are soft, about 5 minutes. Add the celery and quinoa, and sauté for 1 minute to lightly toast.

Turn the sauté off, then add the water, beets, lentils, carrot, bay leaves, marjoram, thyme and basil to your Instant Pot.

Wrap the Romanesco florets in foil and place on top of the stew. This will slow the cooking so they don't get mushy.

Cook on high pressure for 10 minutes and manually release the pressure. Carefully remove and open the foil packet.

Remove the bay leaves. Dish up the stew into four bowls and divide the Romanesco florets between the 4 servings.

WHAT IS ROMANESCO? It's also known as Roman cauliflower, broccolo Romanesco or romanesque cauliflower. It's a stunning chartreuse color and it looks like a fractal come to life. It has a more delicate and nutty flavor than regular cauliflower.

PER SERVING: Calories 95.4, protein 6.5 g, total fat 0.5 g, carbohydrates 18.5 g, sodium 55.6 mg, fiber 6.5 g

Chef AJ's Black Bean and Mushroom Chili

SOY-FREE, OIL-FREE

Makes 10 servings

You guys know I love me some Chef AJ! She is an amazing vegan plant-based chef that cooks for the power of health. This is her famous chili. It makes a lot so you can make it for a potluck or a party, or you can just freeze any leftovers you might have for another time. This is delicious over a baked Yukon Gold potato or brown rice.

Make in a 6-quart or 8-quart (6-L or 8-L) Instant Pot. See the note in directions for the 6-quart option. Cut the recipe in half to make in a 3-quart Instant Pot.

PRESSURE COOKER INGREDIENTS

3 cups (450 g) chopped onions

8 cloves (25 g) garlic, minced or pressed through a garlic press

2 lb (907 g) mushrooms, sliced

3 (15-oz [425-g]) cans salt-free black beans (do not drain) or 4½ cups (774 g) cooked beans

1 lb (454 g) frozen corn, defrosted

1 tbsp (7 g) ground cumin

1 tbsp (5 g) dried oregano

½ tbsp (4 g) smoked paprika

2 tsp (2 g) no-salt chili powder

½ tsp chipotle powder

Salt substitute, to taste

TOPPINGS (OPTIONAL)

No-oil bean cheese (page 41), shredded

Dollop of plain vegan yogurt

Fresh chopped green onions or minced red onions

Place the onions, garlic, mushrooms and black beans including the liquid from the cans in your Instant Pot. If using a 3-quart (3-L) or 8-quart (8-L) Instant Pot, add the corn now; you will add after cooking for the 6-quart (6-L). Add the cumin, oregano, smoked paprika, chili powder and chipotle powder to your electric pressure cooker. Mix well.

Cook on high pressure for 6 minutes. Carefully manually release the pressure. If you are using a 6-quart (6-L) Instant Pot, stir in the corn. Taste and add salt substitute as needed. Add your favorite toppings (if using) and serve.

NOTE: One can of beans is approximately 1½ cups (258 g). If you use cooked beans instead of canned beans, you need to add 1½ cups (355 ml) of water.

FEELING AMBITIOUS? If you like, you can use the sauté function and sauté the onions, garlic and mushrooms first. I found that if I sautéed the veggies I was able to add in the corn to my 6-quart (6-L) before cooking.

PER SERVING: Calories 188.3, protein 11.9 g, total fat 1.2 g, carbohydrates 36.9 g, sodium 8.5 mg, fiber 10.0 g

Jackfruit White Bean Chili

SOY-FREE. OIL-FREE

Makes 6 servings

The jackfruit gives this white chili the perfect texture combined with the Great Northern beans. It's seasoned with mild ancho chili powder, green chilies and ground cumin, but it's the oregano and lime juice that makes it really special.

Make in a 3-quart or 6-quart (3-L or 6-L) Instant Pot. Double and make in your 8-quart (8-L) Instant Pot.

SAUTÉ INGREDIENTS

½ cup (118 ml) water

1 cup (150 g) minced onion

1 tsp minced garlic

1½ tsp (3 g) ground cumin

1½ tsp (1 g) ancho chili powder or your favorite chili powder

PRESSURE COOKER INGREDIENTS

2 (28-oz [794-g]) cans jackfruit in brine, drained and rinsed

3 cups (708 ml) water

4 tbsp (34 g) diced green chilies

1 salt-free bouillon cube

1 lb (454 g) Great Northern beans, soaked at least 8 hours, drained and rinsed

BEFORE SERVING

2 tsp (4 g) Mexican oregano, substitute regular oregano or marjoram

2 tsp (10 ml) lime juice, or to taste

Salt, to taste (optional)

TOPPINGS (OPTIONAL)

Chopped cilantro

Cashew cream

Hot sauce

Jalapeño powder

Jalapeño salt

Turn the sauté function on and heat the water. Once hot, add the onions and cook until translucent, 3 to 5 minutes. Add the garlic, cumin and chili powder. Sauté until the spices become fragrant, about 2 minutes.

Turn the sauté off. Add in the jackfruit, shredding it with your hands. Then stir in the water, green chilies, bouillon cube and soaked beans. Cook on high manual/pressure for 10 minutes. Let the pressure release manually.

Add the oregano, lime juice and salt, to taste (if using).

Serve with your favorite toppings such as cilantro, cashew cream or hot sauce. Sprinkle the bowls with jalapeño powder or jalapeño salt to add an extra flavor burst.

PER SERVING: Calories 391.3, protein 35.1 g, total fat 1.0 g, carbohydrates 114.0 g, sodium 565.8 mg, fiber 66.0 g

102   Gluten-Free, Vegan Cooking in Your Instant Pot®

veggie and grain mains

The Instant Pot is my go-to cooking tool all year round. It cooks brown rice and other whole grains quickly, and it doesn't heat up your house during the summer.

Same goes for vegetables. Many people think they can't pressure cook fresh and delicate veggies, but—as weird as it may sound—you can cook broccoli or asparagus in zero minutes in the Instant Pot! Remember that it starts cooking even as it builds up to pressure.

This chapter brings you hearty recipes with oat groats, fried rice and all-veggie main courses, too. Try tweaking the recipes with seasonal veggies and substitute in some of your favorite grains with similar cooking times.

Be sure to check out the Vegetable Cooking Chart (page 167) and Grain Cooking Chart (page 168) for more details.

Plant-Based Niçoise-Style Potato Salad

SOY-FREE. OIL-FREE. REFINED SUGAR-FREE

Makes 4 servings

I love eating potato salad straight from the fridge on super-hot days, and I bet you do too. The oil-free dressing makes this salad super healthy. Traditional Niçoise has tuna, so you can add some canned chickpeas slightly mashed to add that textural element if you want.

Make in a 3-quart, 6-quart or 8-quart (3-L, 6-L or 8-L) Instant Pot.

1 cup (236 ml) water

4 cups (600 g) quartered baby potatoes

2 cups (220 g) trimmed green beans, cut in half

½ cup (118 ml) aquafaba

1 tbsp (15 ml) balsamic vinegar

2 tsp (10 g) Dijon mustard (or use yellow mustard if that's what you have)

1 tsp apple cider vinegar

½ tsp dried thyme, or 2 tsp (5 g) fresh thyme

¾ tsp granulated garlic

¼ tsp onion powder

¼ tsp salt, or to taste (optional)

⅛ tsp pepper

1 cup (180 g) diced ripe tomatoes or quartered cherry tomatoes

¼ cup (45 g) sliced Kalamata olives or Niçoise olives (optional)

Butter lettuce

Add the water to the electric pressure cooker liner. Put the potatoes in a steamer that fits inside your electric pressure cooker and lower into the liner.

Wrap the green beans in parchment paper and then in foil to slow the cooking process for them. Add the foil packet to the Instant Pot. Cook on high pressure for 6 minutes. Release the pressure manually.

Carefully remove the steamer and foil packet. Run cold water over the potatoes and green bean packet until they are both cool.

Add the aquafaba, balsamic vinegar, mustard, apple cider vinegar, thyme, granulated garlic, onion powder, salt (if using) and pepper to a bowl, blender or food processor. If you're using a bowl, whisk until foamy and thick, or blend or process until it thickens.

Assemble the salad by adding the cooled potatoes and green beans to a large bowl. Add half of the salad dressing and gently mix. Add the tomatoes and olives (if using). Add in more dressing as needed. Serve over lettuce.

Make this into an almost traditional salad by using the steamed potatoes and green beans and using some vegan mayo and mustard to create a traditional dressing. Or mix with your favorite vegan ranch dressing.

PER SERVING: Calories 125.1, protein 3.5 g, total fat 0.1 g, carbohydrates 28.0 g, sodium 88.4 mg, fiber 5.5 g

The Veggie Queen's Broccoli Raab with Shiitake Mushrooms

SOY-FREE.
OIL-FREE OPTION

Makes 4 servings

This recipe comes from my friend, Jill Nussinow, also known as The Veggie Queen. Broccoli raab is also called rabe or rapini and it's not truly broccoli but more like mustard or turnip greens with a slightly bitter edge. Choose only bright green bunches. The mushrooms help tone down the bitter edge and add richness to the dish, as well as a nutrition boost.

Make in a 3-quart or 6-quart (3-L or 6-L) Instant Pot.

SAUTÉ INGREDIENTS

1 tbsp (15 ml) olive oil (or water sauté to make oil-free)

6 shiitake mushrooms, stems removed and saved for stock, sliced thin

PRESSURE COOKER INGREDIENTS

5 cloves garlic, minced

1 bunch broccoli raab, chopped (4 cups [160 g])

Pinch of red pepper flakes (optional)

¼ cup (59 ml) broth, mushroom or vegetable or water with 2 tsp (3 g) dry bouillon (page 28)

Salt, to taste

Turn your Instant Pot to sauté. Heat the olive oil and add the mushrooms. Sauté for 2 minutes or until they start wilting.

Add the garlic, broccoli raab, red pepper flakes (if using) and broth. Set the timer for 2 minutes, on high pressure.

When time is up, quick release the pressure and remove the lid, carefully tilting it away from you. Remove the finished dish to a plate and add salt, to taste. Serve hot.

PER SERVING: Calories 53.5, protein 4.8 g, total fat 0.6 g, carbohydrates 7.5 g, sodium 91.3 mg, fiber 3.6 g

Jackfruit Biryani

Biryani is an Indian rice dish that's one of my all-time favorites. It's hard to get it vegan at the restaurants near me, so I made a vegan version in my Instant Pot. You can change out the jackfruit for cooked chickpeas, reconstituted soy curls or more veggies. Serve with my Vegan Raita (page 112)!

Make in a 3-quart or 6-quart (3-L or 6-L) Instant Pot. Double and make in your 8-quart (8-L) Instant Pot.

SOY-FREE.
OIL-FREE OPTION.
REFINED SUGAR-FREE

Makes 4 servings

JACKFRUIT INGREDIENTS

1½ cups (265 g) jackfruit in brine, drained, rinsed and shredded

¼ tsp ground coriander

¼ tsp ground cumin

⅛ tsp ground cinnamon

⅛ tsp ground turmeric

1/16 tsp red chili powder (optional)

1/16 tsp black pepper

SAUTÉ INGREDIENTS

1 tbsp (14 g) vegan butter or mild oil (or dry sauté to make oil-free)

½ tsp whole cumin seeds

1 cup (150 g) minced onion

1½ tsp (4 g) minced garlic

PRESSURE COOKER INGREDIENTS

2 cups (370 g) long grain brown rice

2 cups (475 ml) water

1½ cups (195 g) chopped carrots

1½ cups (225 g) chopped potatoes

2 tsp (2 g) minced fresh ginger

4 whole cardamom pods

1 whole cinnamon stick

1 bay leaf

BEFORE SERVING

2 cups (300 g) green peas, thawed if frozen

Salt, to taste

Combine the jackfruit with the coriander, ground cumin, cinnamon, turmeric, red chili powder (if using) and pepper. You can make this the night before and store it in the fridge until ready to use.

Turn your Instant Pot sauté setting on low. Add the butter. Once warm, add the cumin seeds and sauté until fragrant, about 1 minute. Add the onion and cook until translucent, about 5 minutes. Add the garlic and sauté for 1 minute. Add the jackfruit mixture. Cook until most of the liquid is cooked off. Turn the sauté off.

Add the rice, water, carrots, potatoes, ginger, cardamom pods, cinnamon stick and bay leaf. Cook on high pressure for 24 minutes. Let the pressure release naturally for 10 minutes, then manually release the rest of the pressure.

Remove the cinnamon stick, cardamom pods and bay leaf. Stir in the peas. They will heat up enough on the warm setting. Salt to taste and serve warm.

PER SERVING: Calories 256.6, protein 8.2 g, total fat 1.3 g, carbohydrates 53.4 g, sodium 241.5 mg, fiber 10.9 g

(continued)

VEGAN RAITA RECIPE

Raita is a savory yogurt sauce that goes great on biryani. It's also tasty on any Indian curries or stews.

1 cup (236 ml) unsweetened plain vegan yogurt

1 medium cucumber, seeded and diced small

½ tsp ground cumin

Salt, to taste

Mix all of the ingredients together and serve on the side of the Jackfruit Biryani. Store leftovers in the fridge.

PER SERVING: Calories 14.1, protein 0.6 g, total fat 0.9 g, carbohydrates 1.0 g, sodium 1.3 mg, fiber 0.4 g

Nancie's Green Curry Sweet Potatoes with Shiitake Mushrooms

SOY-FREE OPTION.
OIL-FREE

Makes 6 servings

If you had told me you could make your own green curry paste with ingredients from the regular grocery store, I would not have believed you. But Nancie McDermott is the queen of Southern food and she is passionate about Thai food—and she made me into a believer. You can certainly buy premade green curry paste if you'd rather. Either way, this creamy coconut curry with sweet potatoes and shiitakes will elevate your dinner with flavors worthy of a Thai restaurant.

Make in a 3-quart or 6-quart (3-L or 6-L) Instant Pot. Double and make in your 8-quart (8-L) Instant Pot.

1½ cups (355 ml) full-fat coconut milk, stirred well, divided

½ cup (56 g) fresh Green Curry Paste (page 115), or 3 tbsp (45 g) store-bought green curry paste

1 sweet potato (114 g), peeled and cut into 2-inch (5-cm) chunks (or substitute butternut squash, Hubbard squash or kabocha pumpkin)

1½ cups (130 g) sliced shiitake mushrooms or button mushrooms (¼ inch [6 mm] thick)

½ cup (118 ml) water

2 tsp (10 ml) pure maple syrup or sweetener of choice, to taste (optional)

2 tsp (11 g) fine sea salt

1 cup (120 g) frozen edamame beans (use frozen green peas to make soy-free)

3 tbsp (19 g) finely chopped green onion

Cooked grain or gluten-free noodles

Chopped fresh cilantro

On your Instant Pot, press sauté and add about half of the coconut milk. Stir often as the coconut milk steams, becomes fragrant and reaches a gentle but active boil, 1 to 2 minutes.

Add the curry paste and cook, stirring and pressing occasionally, to dissolve the curry paste into the coconut milk, about 1 minute. Add the sweet potato and mushrooms. Stir to mix well and coat them with the sauce.

Press cancel to stop the cooking cycle. Add the remaining coconut milk, water, maple syrup (if using) and sea salt. Stir well. Cook on high pressure for 6 minutes.

When the cooking cycle is complete, let the pressure naturally release for 3 minutes, then manually release the rest of the pressure.

Stir in the frozen edamame and green onion. Taste and adjust any seasonings as needed. Serve the curry hot or warm over the grain of your choice or over gluten-free noodles. Garnish with the cilantro. Store leftovers in an airtight container in the fridge for up to 1 week.

PER SERVING: Calories 220.1, protein 5.6 g, total fat 15.0 g, carbohydrates 16.6 g, sodium 196.1 mg, fiber 1.7 g

(continued)

GREEN CURRY PASTE

It's powerful being able to make your own Thai curry paste. Why? You can make sure everything that goes in fits in your diet. Nancie's version below is not only vegan but oil-free as well!

Makes about 1½ cups (170 g)

5–7 fresh green jalapeño chilies

¾ cup (12 g) coarsely chopped fresh cilantro or parsley

½ cup (75 g) chopped shallots or onion

⅓ cup (30 g) peeled and coarsely chopped fresh ginger

2 tbsp (16 g) chopped garlic

1 tsp ground cumin

1 tsp ground coriander

½ tsp ground pepper

⅓–½ cup (78–118 ml) water, divided

To prepare the jalapeño chilies, trim away the stem end and cut in half lengthwise. Carefully remove and discard the seeds, leaving only the green chilies. Coarsely chop and measure ⅔ cup (about 60 g); reserve any extra for another recipe.

In a blender or small food processor, combine the chilies, cilantro, shallots, ginger, garlic, cumin, coriander and pepper. Add ⅓ cup (78 ml) of the water and process for 1 minute.

Stop to scrape down the sides and then continue processing, pulsing and stopping to scrape down as needed, until you have a fairly smooth, very well-combined puree. Add more water as needed to move the blades and transform chunky ingredients into a smooth paste or sauce.

Transfer to a jar, cover and refrigerate for up to 1 week, or freeze for 1 month.

PER SERVING: Calories 8.3, protein 0.3 g, total fat 0.1 g, carbohydrates 1.8 g, sodium 1.0 mg, fiber 0.2 g

Jamaican Jackfruit with Curry

I love Jamaican food, so I asked Michelle Blackwood of healthiersteps.com to contribute one of her flavorful curries. This one is made with potatoes and jackfruit and has gluten-free dumplings to make it even heartier!

Make in a 6-quart (6-L) Instant Pot. Double the recipe to make in an 8-quart (8-L) Instant Pot or cut it in half to make in a 3-quart (3-L) Instant Pot.

SOY-FREE, OIL-FREE OPTION, REFINED SUGAR-FREE

Makes 8 servings

½ cup (60 g) gluten-free flour

Salt, to taste

¼ cup + 2 tbsp (90 ml) water

2 tbsp (30 g) coconut oil (or use water sauté to make oil-free)

2 tbsp (10 g) Easy Jamaican Curry Powder (page 53)

1 tsp paprika

1 tsp ground cumin

1 tsp ground turmeric

2 sprigs of fresh thyme or 1 tsp dried

1 cup (150 g) minced onion

4 cloves garlic, minced

1 tsp fresh grated ginger

2 green onions, chopped

1 (20-oz [567-g]) can green jackfruit, drained and rinsed

4 potatoes (about 692 g), cubed

1 medium (60 g) carrot, diced

1 (15-oz [443-ml]) can coconut milk

2 cups (475 ml) vegetable broth

1 tsp Italian seasoning

¼–½ tsp cayenne pepper

¼ cup (4 g) chopped cilantro

Salt, to taste (optional)

To prepare the dumplings, combine the flour and salt in a medium bowl. Add the water and mix to combine. Knead the dough to form a smooth ball. Take a small piece of dough and roll it between the palms of your hands to form a cylindrical shape or ball. Repeat to form 16 dumplings. Set aside for later.

Turn your Instant Pot to sauté. Add the oil. When it is hot, add the curry powder, paprika, cumin, turmeric and thyme. Cook for a minute, stirring constantly. Add the onion, garlic, ginger and green onions. Cook for 2 minutes, or until the onions are soft. Add the jackfruit, potatoes and carrot. Stir to coat.

Turn the sauté off. Add the coconut milk, vegetable broth, Italian seasoning and cayenne pepper, and drop the dumplings on top of the curry. Stir to mix everything together.

Cook on high pressure for 10 minutes. Let the pressure release naturally for 10 minutes, then manually release the pressure the rest of the way.

Remove the lid. Stir in the cilantro and crush some of the potatoes to thicken the curry. Add salt to taste (if using) and adjust any seasonings as needed.

You can buy premade Jamaican curry powder, but be sure to carefully check the ingredients. Some of the blends contain wheat flour or gluten. Jamaican curry powder is very different from garam masala or other Indian curry blends. It's more yellow from the turmeric. And even though it uses some of the same spices, the ratio of them makes all the difference.

PER SERVING: Calories 135.1, protein 2.6 g, total fat 0.3 g, carbohydrates 30.2 g, sodium 175.3 mg, fiber 7.0 g

Hungarian-Style Cabbage "Noodles"

To be upfront, the noodles in this are actually strips of cabbage. This is a great way to use up extra cabbage and Brussels sprouts from your CSA box. It's also a great way to have a filling all-vegetable dinner in the cooler weather when I tend to rely too much on heavy grains and pasta. Serve this with tofu steak or braised tempeh and potatoes to round out the meal.

Make in a 3-quart or 6-quart (3-L or 6-L) Instant Pot. Double and make in your 8-quart (8-L) Instant Pot.

SOY-FREE.
OIL-FREE OPTION.
REFINED SUGAR-FREE

Makes 4 servings
as a side

SAUTÉ INGREDIENTS

1 tbsp (14 g) vegan butter (or about ¼ cup [60 ml] water to make oil-free)

½ cup (75 g) minced onion

8 oz (227 g) mushrooms, sliced

1 tsp minced garlic

2 tsp (4 g) smoked paprika

1 tsp caraway seeds

PRESSURE COOKER INGREDIENTS

4 cups (280 g) red cabbage "noodles," cut ¼ inch (6 mm) thick

2 cups (200 g) shredded Brussels sprouts or substitute green cabbage

½ cup (118 ml) water

1 tsp dried dill

BEFORE SERVING

Salt and pepper, to taste

Chopped fresh dill (optional)

Turn your Instant Pot sauté setting on low. Add the butter and cook the onion until translucent, about 8 minutes. Add the mushrooms, garlic, smoked paprika and caraway seeds. Sauté for 5 minutes, or until the mushrooms begin to release their liquid.

Turn the sauté off. Add the red cabbage, Brussels sprouts, water and dill to your Instant Pot. Cook on high pressure for 5 minutes and release the pressure manually.

Before serving add salt and pepper, to taste. Garnish with fresh dill (if using).

PER SERVING: Calories 151.4, protein 7.2 g, total fat 5.6 g, carbohydrates 23.7 g, sodium 56.2 mg, fiber 6.7 g

Butternut Oat Groat Risotto

SOY-FREE. OIL-FREE. REFINED SUGAR-FREE

Makes 4 servings

Oat groats are whole oats that just have the inedible husk removed. They make this risotto extra creamy. This is the recipe you want to share at a Thanksgiving dinner with friends or family.

Make in a 3-quart or 6-quart (3-L or 6-L) Instant Pot. Double and make in your 8-quart (8-L) Instant Pot.

SAUTÉ INGREDIENTS

1 tbsp (15 ml) olive oil (or water sauté to make oil-free)

½ cup (75 g) minced onion

1 tsp minced garlic

PRESSURE COOKER FIRST COOK INGREDIENTS

3 cups (708 ml) water

2 cups (336 g) oat groats, rinsed and drained

2 vegan bouillon cubes or 1 tbsp (5 g) dry bouillon (page 28)

1 tsp DIY Poultry Seasoning (page 50)

PRESSURE COOKER SECOND COOK INGREDIENTS

2 cups (280 g) chopped butternut squash

1 cup (236 ml) water, if needed

BEFORE SERVING

2 packed cups (134 g) chopped mild greens, such as kale, collards or spinach

2 tbsp (12 g) nutritional yeast

Salt and pepper, to taste

TOPPINGS (OPTIONAL)

Fresh thyme

Vegan feta

Vegan Parmesan

Fresh julienned greens

Toasted pumpkin seeds

Turn your Instant Pot to sauté. Add the oil and cook the onion until translucent, 3 to 5 minutes. Add the garlic and sauté for 1 minute.

Turn the sauté off. Add the water, oat groats, bouillon and poultry seasoning to your Instant Pot. Cook on high pressure for 45 minutes and manually release the pressure. Stir in the butternut squash and add up to an additional cup (236 ml) of water if the mixture is dry. Remember you will need to have at least ¼ cup (59 ml) of liquid left for the Instant Pot to come back up to pressure.

Close and cook on high pressure for 15 minutes. Manually release the pressure. If there's extra liquid, switch to the sauté mode and cook it off.

Stir in the greens; it will cook from the heat of the stew. Add the nutritional yeast, salt and pepper until it's just right for you.

You can serve this on a platter and top with fresh thyme, vegan feta and Parmesan, julienned greens and/or pumpkin seeds (if using). Or you can add bowls of toppings for you and your guests to add as you like.

PER SERVING: Calories 237.1, protein 10.9 g, total fat 3.6 g, carbohydrates 45.7 g, sodium 24.0 mg, fiber 19.5 g

Soy Curl Fried Rice with Lots of Options

SOY-FREE OPTION.
OIL-FREE OPTION.
REFINED SUGAR-FREE

Makes 4 servings

Since going gluten-free, I miss going to my neighborhood Chinese restaurant. Soy sauce has gluten in it and most Chinese dishes have soy sauce. That means there's not much for me there anymore. But that's okay—I'll just make my own Asian dishes in my Instant Pot. This fried rice can be made with lots of different veggies or proteins to suit the season or what's in your kitchen. Just remember that you should add quick-cooking veggies, such as greens, peas or broccoli, just before serving to keep them from getting mushy.

Make in a 3-quart or 6-quart (3-L or 6-L) Instant Pot. Double and make in your 8-quart (8-L) Instant Pot.

SAUTÉ INGREDIENTS

1 tbsp (15 ml) mild oil (or use water to make oil-free)

1 cup (150 g) minced onion

2 cups (220 g) shredded carrots

2 cups (80 g) dried soy curls, broken into small pieces, reconstituted and drained (or 3 cups [500 g] cubed tofu, 3 cups [500 g] crumbled tempeh, 3 cups [465 g] edamame or 3 cups [500 g] cooked chickpeas)

SAUCE INGREDIENTS

⅓ cup (78 ml) gluten-free tamari (or gluten-free soy sauce, Bragg Liquid Aminos or coconut aminos)

2 tsp (5 g) fresh grated ginger

1 tsp minced garlic

PRESSURE COOKER INGREDIENTS

2 cups (370 g) long grain brown rice

2 cups (475 ml) water

BEFORE SERVING

2 cups (300 g) green peas, thawed if frozen

Turn your Instant Pot sauté setting on low. Add the oil and cook the onion until translucent, about 8 minutes. Add the carrots and soy curls. Cook until most of the liquid is cooked off, about 3 to 5 minutes. Turn the sauté off.

Mix together the tamari, ginger and garlic. Pour the sauce over the cooked mixture and stir. Add the rice and water. Cook on high pressure for 24 minutes. Let the pressure release naturally for 10 minutes, then manually release the rest of the pressure.

Stir in the peas. They will heat up enough on the warm setting. Serve once warm.

PER SERVING: Calories 272.4, protein 14.1 g, total fat 4.3 g, carbohydrates 45.3 g, sodium 132.3 mg, fiber 9.2 g

layered meals and egg mold recipes

Don't worry about the word egg in describing the silicone molds that we use to bake in our Instant Pot. There will be no eggs in this very vegan book. The closest we come is making tofu breakfast bites.

Some people have been able to use the silicone molds without oil. If the brand you buy ends up sticking, you can still use mini muffin papers in them to help without adding oil.

There are a lot of different ways to cook layered meals in your Instant Pot. There are lots of stackable stainless pans used to cook pot in pot. Just keep in mind that you can use those to cook two recipes at once, but it does slow the cooking time of both.

In this book, I'm using one stainless pan over a 2-inch (5-cm) rack. When you're cooking beans, grains and stews together, you don't need to cover the top dish. That allows the two dishes to cook quicker than in the double covered pans.

New Orleans–Style Red Beans with Dirty Brown Rice

SOY-FREE OPTION.
OIL-FREE OPTION

Makes 4 servings

These creamy red beans have a Cajun flair and some sausage flavors over smoky brown rice full of mushroom umami. It's the perfect meal for a Mardi Gras party, but it's good any time of the year!

Make in a 6-quart or 8-quart (6-L or 8-L) Instant Pot.

1 tbsp (15 ml) olive oil (or water sauté to make oil-free)

1 cup (150 g) minced onion

2 tsp (6 g) minced garlic

2 cups (150 g) minced mushrooms, divided

1 cup (150 g) chopped bell pepper

4 cups (944 ml) water or broth

1½ cups (276 g) unsoaked kidney beans or small red beans, rinsed and drained

2 tsp (4 g) DIY Cajun Seasoning Blend (page 49)

½ tsp smoked paprika

½ tsp dried thyme

½ tsp dried oregano

½ tsp dried basil

¼ tsp fennel seeds

2¼ cups (531 ml) water

2 cups (370 g) long grain brown rice

1 vegan bouillon cube

½ tsp liquid smoke

Salt or salt substitute, to taste

Turn your Instant Pot to sauté. Add the oil and cook the onion until translucent, 3 to 5 minutes. Add the garlic, half of the mushrooms and bell pepper, then sauté for about 5 minutes.

Turn the sauté off. Add in the water, beans, Cajun seasoning, smoked paprika, thyme, oregano, basil and fennel seeds to your Instant Pot.

Place a rack with 2- to 3-inch (5- to 7.5-cm) legs into the mixture. This is not the rack that came with your pressure cooker.

You can then put a 4- to 5-cup (960-ml to 1.2-L) Pyrex container or one of the stainless bowls from the stackables you can buy for your Instant Pot on top of the rack.

Use a 5-cup (1.2-L) container that fits on top of the rack and allows the lid to close. Combine the water, brown rice, the rest of the mushrooms, bouillon cube and liquid smoke in the container. Whisk well. You will not cover or put a lid or foil on this.

Cook on high pressure for 35 minutes. Let the pressure release naturally for 10 minutes and manually release the pressure the rest of the way. Carefully remove the top container and set on a trivet. Fluff and mix the rice with a large fork.

Check to make sure the beans are fully cooked; if not, place the lid back on and cook for 10 minutes. Taste and add salt or salt substitute as needed to both dishes.

Serve the creamy beans on top of or beside the dirty rice.

PER SERVING: Calories 277.0, protein 17.0 g, total fat 1.0 g, carbohydrates 59.0 g, sodium 3.5 mg, fiber 10.7 g

Spicy Peanut Butter Tempeh and Collards and Jollof Quinoa

SOY-FREE OPTION.
OIL-FREE OPTION.
REFINED SUGAR-FREE

Makes 6 servings

The tempeh in this dish is creamy with a little heat, and the quinoa is full of flavor and veggies. You're going to love it!

Make in a 3-quart or 6-quart (3-L or 6-L) Instant Pot.

1 tbsp (15 ml) olive oil (or water sauté to make oil-free)

1 cup (150 g) minced onion

2 tsp (6 g) minced garlic

3 cups (708 ml) water or broth

2 cups (340 g) quinoa, rinsed and drained

2 cups (220 g) chopped green beans

1 (28-oz [794-g]) can crushed tomatoes

1½ cups (195 g) diced carrots

1 tbsp (7 g) fresh grated ginger

1 tsp dried thyme

1 tsp paprika

½ tsp cayenne pepper

1 cup (236 ml) water

½ cup (130 g) peanut butter

1 tbsp (7 g) fresh grated ginger

½ tsp cayenne pepper

2 tbsp (30 ml) tomato paste

3 cups (110 g) collards or other mild greens, torn into small pieces

1 (8-oz [227-g]) package tempeh, cut into small cubes (for soy-free, substitute hemp tofu)

Salt or salt substitute, to taste

Turn your Instant Pot to sauté. Add the oil and cook the onion until translucent, 3 to 5 minutes. Add the garlic and sauté for about 3 minutes.

Turn the sauté off. Add in the water, quinoa, green beans, tomatoes, carrots, ginger, thyme, paprika and cayenne pepper to your Instant Pot.

Place a rack with 2- to 3-inch (5- to 7.5-cm) legs into the mixture. This is not the rack that came with your pressure cooker. You can then place a 4- to 5-cup (960-ml to 1.2-L) Pyrex container or one of the stainless bowls from the stackables you can buy for your Instant Pot.

In a mixing bowl, add the water, peanut butter, ginger, cayenne pepper and tomato paste. Add the collards and tempeh, and mix thoroughly. Add the mixture to a 4- to 5-cup (960-ml to 1.2-L) container that fits on top of the rack and allows the lid to close.

Cook on high pressure for 4 minutes and manually release the pressure. Carefully remove the top container and set on a trivet. Taste and add salt or salt substitute as needed to both dishes.

Serve the quinoa mixture and the tempeh mixture next to each other. Enjoy!

Shouldn't we be using Scotch bonnet pepper in this? Yes, it's true. If you like it spicy and they are available, you can add seeded and minced Scotch bonnet pepper in place of the ground peppers. Feel free to make it as hot and scorchy as you like it!

PER SERVING: Calories 603.1, protein 27.3 g, total fat 19.7 g, carbohydrates 85.3 g, sodium 592.7 mg, fiber 15.0 g

Polenta Topped
with Cannellini Bean Stew

SOY-FREE OPTION.
OIL-FREE OPTION

Makes 4 servings

This is cooked in two layers at the same time. The polenta will seize up a little during the cooking process, but all you need to do is whisk it again to make it the perfect texture.

Make in a 3-quart or 6-quart (3-L or 6-L) Instant Pot. Double and make in your 8-quart (8-L) Instant Pot.

1 tbsp (15 ml) olive oil (or water sauté to make oil-free), plus 2 tsp (10 ml) olive oil (optional)

½ cup (75 g) minced onion

2 tsp (6 g) minced garlic

3 cups (708 ml) water or broth

1½ cups (276 g) dry cannellini or Great Northern beans, soaked overnight, drained and rinsed

1 packed tbsp (4 g) minced sun-dried tomatoes

1 tsp dried oregano

1 tsp dried basil

½ tsp dried thyme

1 bay leaf

4 cups (944 ml) water

1 cup (160 g) polenta

¼ cup (24 g) nutritional yeast

2 cups (134 g) chopped kale

Salt or salt substitute, to taste

Turn your Instant Pot to sauté. Add 1 tablespoon (15 ml) of oil and cook the onion until translucent, 3 to 5 minutes. Add the garlic and sauté for about 3 minutes.

Turn the sauté off. Add in the water, soaked beans, sun-dried tomatoes, oregano, basil, thyme and bay leaf to your Instant Pot. Place a rack with 2- to 3-inch (5- to 7.5-cm) legs into the mixture. This is not the rack that came with your pressure cooker.

You can then place a 4- to 5-cup (960-ml to 1.2-L) Pyrex container or one of the stainless bowls from the stackables you can buy for your Instant Pot. Use a 4- to 5-cup (960-ml to 1.2-L) container that fits on top of the rack and allows the lid to close. In the container, combine the water, polenta, nutritional yeast and 2 teaspoons (10 ml) of olive oil (if using). Whisk well. You will not cover or put a lid or foil on this.

Cook on high pressure for 25 minutes. Let the pressure release naturally for 10 minutes and manually release the pressure the rest of the way.

Carefully remove the top container and set on a trivet. Whisk and whisk some more and the polenta will be the perfect texture.

Check to make sure the beans are fully cooked; if not, place the lid back on and cook for 5 minutes. Remove the bay leaf. Stir the kale into the beans, and add salt as needed to both dishes.

Serve the white beans on a bed of polenta.

PER SERVING: Calories 442.1, protein 25.7 g, total fat 1.2 g, carbohydrates 83.1 g, sodium 53.4 mg, fiber 17.5 g

Mini Vegan Corn Dogs

These little bites remind me of my childhood, and they are a fun treat for parties and potlucks. I make mine ahead of time and heat them up in the oven or air fryer to get them crispy.

Make in a 3-quart, 6-quart or 8-quart (3-L, 6-L or 8-L) Instant Pot.

SOY-FREE OPTION.
OIL-FREE. REFINED
SUGAR-FREE

Makes 14 mini
corn dog bites

PRESSURE COOKER INGREDIENTS

1½ cups (355 ml) water

CORN DOG INGREDIENTS

Cooking spray (optional)

2 tbsp (20 g) ground flaxseed mixed with ¼ cup (59 ml) warm water

1½ cups (355 ml) soy milk or other nondairy milk mixed with 2 tbsp (30 ml) apple cider vinegar

2 cups (300 g) fine ground cornmeal

1½ tsp (7 g) baking powder

¼ tsp salt

3 vegan, gluten-free hot dogs, cut into 6 pieces each

FOR SERVING (OPTIONAL)

Dipping sauces, such as ketchup, mustard, Sriracha or barbecue sauce

NOTE: For this recipe, you need 2 egg bite molds or 14 (2 tablespoon–sized) ramekins. The 3-quart (3-L) egg bite molds hold 4 at a time, so you will need to make the recipe in batches.

Add the water to the pressure cooker liner. Oil the egg bite molds or small ramekins with cooking spray, if using.

Add the flaxseed mixture to the soy milk mixture. Stir well. In a mixing bowl, combine the cornmeal, baking powder and salt. Pour in the wet mixture and stir well.

Put 1 tablespoon (15 ml) of batter into the bottom of the mold and tap on the counter to even out the batter. Press in a piece of hot dog and top with a second tablespoon (15 ml) of batter. Once again tap the mold on the counter to even out the batter.

Cover with foil or the plastic lid that came with your mold. Repeat with the second mold.

You can lower the molds down using the rack that came with your Instant Pot. I also recommend using an OXO sling or making handles out of aluminum foil (page 159) to make it easier to get them out later.

Place the rack or sling with the molds in your Instant Pot. Cook on high pressure for 15 minutes and manually release the pressure.

Carefully remove the rack from the Instant Pot and set on your stovetop or a trivet to cool. Turn over the mold and use the finger indent to get the bite to pop out. Serve with dipping sauces (if using).

Make this soy-free by skipping the dogs and adding a teaspoon of Mayocoba Refried Beans (page 88) in their place. It's almost like a tamale bite. Serve with salsa, guacamole and/or barbecue sauce.

PER 1 MINI CORN DOG BITE: Calories 82.5, protein 4.1 g, total fat 1.7 g, carbohydrates 14.1 g, sodium 81.4 mg, fiber 2.3 g

Tofu Breakfast Bites

These little bites are full of eggy flavor from the kala namak, an Indian salt that has a lot of sulfur, also known as black salt. If you are salt-free I'd recommend using some garam masala to spice them up. This recipe uses an egg bite silicone accessory or you can use small ramekins.

SOY-FREE. OIL-FREE. REFINED SUGAR-FREE

Makes 14 tofu bites in the 7-hole molds

Make in a 3-quart, 6-quart or 8-quart (3-L, 6-L or 8-L) Instant Pot.

1 (12-oz [340-g]) box shelf-stable silken tofu

1 (8-oz [227-g]) package super firm tofu (high protein)

¼ cup (24 g) nutritional yeast

1–2 tsp (3 g) kala namak, or to taste (optional)

½ tsp ground turmeric

½ tsp dried marjoram

¼–½ tsp black pepper, or to taste

¼ tsp smoked paprika

⅛ tsp granulated garlic

1½ cups (355 ml) water

NOTE: You can cook all 14 by layering two molds or cook 7 at a time if you have one mold. If you use small mini muffins, take note of how much filling you use in one and adjust the number it will make from there. Also note, the accessory for a 3-quart (3-L) only makes 4 bites at a time, so you will need to make the recipe in batches.

Add the silken tofu, super firm tofu, nutritional yeast, kala namak (if using), turmeric, marjoram, black pepper, smoked paprika and granulated garlic to your blender or food processor. Blend until smooth, stopping a few times to scrape down the blender.

Add the water to the bottom of your electric pressure cooker liner. If you are using an 8-quart (8-L) Instant Pot, use 2 cups (475 ml) of water.

Lightly oil the inside of the mold or use mini cupcake papers to make it oil-free. Divide the mixture to evenly fill the holes in the mold. Cover the egg bite mold with foil.

You can lower the bowl down using the handles of the rack that came with your Instant Pot. I also recommend using an OXO sling or making handles out of aluminum foil (page 159) to make it easier to get it out later.

Cook on high pressure for 20 minutes. Then manually release the rest of the pressure. Remove the mold from the electric pressure cooker and set on a trivet.

Once it's cool enough to handle, remove the foil and place a cutting board on top of the mold. Carefully flip it so that the mold is upside down on top of the cutting board. Give the mold a little shake and the bites should drop to the cutting board. Serve warm or cold.

Make this salt-free by leaving out the kala namak and adding in your favorite salt substitute or salt-free seasoning blend. Kala namak is sometimes called black salt even though it's pink. You can find it on Amazon or in Indian markets.

PER 1 BREAKFAST BITE: Calories 33.3, protein 4.4 g, total fat 1.5 g, carbohydrates 1.5 g, sodium 17.1 mg, fiber 0.2 g

Banana Walnut Mini Muffins

There's something fun about making muffins in your Instant Pot. Even though these have no oil, they are extra moist. In fact, they are so moist that I recommend letting them cool on a cake-cooling rack to get rid of the excess moisture before you eat them.

Make in a 3-quart, 6-quart or 8-quart (3-L, 6-L or 8-L) Instant Pot.

SOY-FREE, OIL-FREE, REFINED SUGAR-FREE OPTION

Makes 14 mini muffins

DRY INGREDIENTS

1¼ cups (150 g) gluten-free baking blend

1¾ tsp (8 g) baking powder

Pinch of salt

⅓ cup (42 g) chopped walnuts

WET INGREDIENTS

1¼ cups (280 g) ripe bananas

½ cup (118 ml) unsweetened nondairy milk

¼ cup (59 ml) maple or date syrup, or to taste

NOTE: This recipe uses 2 silicone egg bite molds or a silicone mini muffin accessory. Or you can use small ramekins. Also note, the accessory for a 3-quart (3-L) only makes 4 bites at a time, so you will need to make the recipe in batches.

If you only have one egg bite mold, cut this recipe in half or cook it two separate times.

Mix the gluten-free baking blend, baking powder, salt and walnuts in a bowl.

Mash the bananas in a 4-cup (944-ml) measuring cup. I use a potato masher. In the same measuring cup, add the nondairy milk and sweetener of your choice. Mix well. If your bananas are very ripe and sweet, you can start with half the amount of sweetener in this step, then adjust at the very end.

Add the wet ingredients to the dry and mix well. Add 1½ cups (355 ml) of water to the bottom of your electric pressure cooker liner. If you are using an 8-quart (8-L), use 2 cups (475 ml) of water.

Lightly oil the inside of the molds or use mini cupcake papers to make it oil-free. Divide the mixture to evenly fill the holes in the molds. Cover the silicone molds with foil. Stack on top of one another, making sure the holes do not line up.

You can lower the bowl down using the rack that came with your electric pressure cooker. I also recommend using an OXO sling or making handles out of aluminum foil (page 159) to make it easier to get it out later.

Cook on high pressure for 12 minutes, then manually release the rest of the pressure. Remove the mold from the electric pressure cooker and set on a trivet. Once it's cool enough to handle, remove the foil and place a cutting board on top of the mold. Carefully flip it so that the mold is upside down on top of the cutting board.

Give the mold a little shake and the bites should drop to the cutting board. Place each mini muffin on a cooling rack. This helps them dry out a bit and keep their shape better.

PER SERVING: Calories 92.6, protein 1.4 g, total fat 2.5 g, carbohydrates 17.3 g, sodium 69.9 mg, fiber 1.1 g

breakfast

I alternate between my favorite breakfasts during the week, going back and forth between the Sweet Potato Spice Breakfast Oat Groats (page 147) and Ashley's Dark Chocolate Quinoa Porridge (page 148). I recommend making one batch of each over the weekend. Keep out what you will use for three days and freeze the rest in single servings.

Also use the recipe for Steel-Cut Oats Cooked with Earl Grey Tea (page 143) as a base to create your own seasonal steel-cut oat recipes. Mix and match water, tea or nondairy milk, plus flavorings, fruits and veggies. You can do the same with the chocolate quinoa by varying the fresh fruit topping.

Veggies for Breakfast

Veggies for breakfast? I have to admit that I heard about purposely eating veggies for breakfast from Chef AJ. I was skeptical at first, but once I spent a week eating them for the first meal of my day, I felt better and I was able to get more greens in my diet with little thought.

GREENS

Leafy greens without stems can be cooked for 0 minutes on high pressure. If you add the thick stems, slice them and tear the tender leaves from them, then cook for 2 to 3 minutes on high pressure. Try seasoning with liquid smoke or smoked paprika. It's an old Southern tradition to add a little apple cider vinegar to bitter greens to mellow them out a bit.

GREENS WITH OTHER VEGGIES

When cooking greens, don't forget that you can add in some quick-cooking vegetables such as broccoli, green peas, snap peas, corn, shredded carrot and summer squash. You can also throw in some pre-cooked longer cooking veggies, too. I like to use up leftover vegetables from dinner that way. Season with your favorite salt-free blend, chili powder or other seasoning blend to switch it up with little effort.

VEGETABLE GRITS

This is one of my new favorite breakfasts. You can make this with the Rainbow Vegetable Rice (page 45). My favorite is to use cauliflower. Be sure to try them with carrots, parsnips or sweet potatoes, too.

The difference between vegetable rice and vegetable grits is the grits are processed smaller in your food processor. You can start with cauliflower rice from your freezer or use a whole head of cauliflower. Refer to page 167 if you are starting with a whole head.

To make the vegetable grits, mix in some smoked paprika, nutritional yeast, salt substitute and just enough unsweetened nondairy milk to moisten them. Add water to the bottom of your Instant Pot and put the rack that came with it in the bottom. Place the grits into a Pyrex or stainless steel container that fits into your Instant Pot. Cook on high pressure for 1 minute.

SWEET POTATOES

These are always my favorites—any way and anytime. I cook up a few pounds of sweet potatoes at a time to keep in the fridge. You can always cut the cooked ones into "toast" slices. I like to air fry mine until crispy, but you can do the same thing on sauté in your Instant Pot or in your oven.

POTATOES

Home fries anyone? I cut potatoes into small chunks and cover them with water. Cook them on high pressure for 5 minutes. Drain, then either sauté in your Instant Pot until golden brown or use an air fryer or your oven.

Steel-Cut Oats Cooked with Earl Grey Tea

SOY-FREE, OIL-FREE, REFINED SUGAR-FREE

Makes 4 servings

Don't let the 3-minute cooking time fool you, there is extra time involved in building up pressure and waiting for the pressure to come down. For the easiest breakfast, put the tea and oats in your Instant Pot before you go to sleep and set the timer to start about 30 minutes before you want to leave the house.

Make in a 3-quart or 6-quart (3-L or 6-L) Instant Pot. Double and make in your 8-quart (8-L) Instant Pot.

PRESSURE COOKER INGREDIENTS

3 cups (708 ml) brewed Earl Grey Tea; you can use black, decaf or rooibos

1 cup (161 g) steel-cut oats

BEFORE SERVING

1 tsp rosewater, vanilla extract or a few drops of lavender extract

Sweetener of choice, to taste

Nondairy milk

Add the brewed tea and oats to your Instant Pot. Cook on the manual/pressure cooking setting for 3 minutes. Allow the pressure to release naturally.

Open and mix in an extra flavoring and your choice of sweetener. Serve topped with nondairy milk.

PER SERVING: Calories 158.0, total fat 3.0 g, sodium 3.0 mg, carbohydrates 28.0 g, fiber 4.0 g, sugar 1.0 g, protein 5.0 g

Tofu or Chickpea Shakshuka

SOY-FREE. OIL-FREE.
REFINED SUGAR-FREE

Makes 4 servings

This is a flavorful and filling breakfast or brunch. It's really a spiced tomato and vegetable stew studded with yummy bites of tofu. Set out a table with all the toppings and let your guests dress them up any way they like it! The flavorful tomato base is always a winner.

Make in a 3-quart or 6-quart (3-L or 6-L) Instant Pot. Double and make in your 8-quart (8-L) Instant Pot.

SAUTÉ INGREDIENTS

1 tbsp (15 ml) oil (or water sauté to make oil-free)

1 cup (150 g) minced onion

1 tsp minced garlic

1 cup (150 g) chopped bell pepper

PRESSURE COOKER INGREDIENTS

1 (28-oz [794-g]) can crushed tomatoes

½ cup (118 ml) water

1 (1-lb [454-g]) package super firm tofu cut into cubes or 3 cups (500 g) cooked chickpeas

1 cup (130 g) chopped carrots

1 tsp ground cumin

1 tsp ground coriander

1 tsp dried oregano

1 tsp smoked paprika

BEFORE SERVING

2 packed cups (134 g) chopped kale

Salt and pepper, to taste

Cayenne pepper or other hot pepper powder, to taste

FOR SERVING

Chopped parsley

Vegan feta cheese (optional)

Toasted gluten-free bread

Turn your Instant Pot to sauté. Add the oil and cook the onion until translucent, 3 to 5 minutes. Add the garlic and bell pepper, and sauté for 5 minutes.

Turn the sauté off. Add the tomatoes, water, tofu, carrots, cumin, coriander, oregano and paprika to your Instant Pot. Cook on high pressure for 10 minutes and manually release the pressure.

Stir in the kale; it will cook from the heat of the stew. Add the salt, pepper and cayenne pepper until it's just right for you. Top with parsley and crumbled vegan cheese (if using), and serve with toasted gluten-free bread to soak up all the broth.

You can even make this into a veggies-for-breakfast or brunch dish. Leave out the tofu or chickpeas and cook the tomato mixture for 10 minutes. Then add 3 to 5 cups (weight will vary) of quick-cooking veggies, such as broccoli, cauliflower and summer squash. Cook on sauté or cook for 1 minute on high pressure.

PER SERVING: Calories 239.4, protein 22.8 g, total fat 5.3 g, carbohydrates 30.2 g, sodium 400.4 mg, fiber 7.4 g

Sweet Potato Spice Breakfast Oat Groats

Oat groats are becoming popular again. What's not to like about a healthy whole grain that fills you up? This recipe has all the flavors of sweet potato casserole, but in a healthy breakfast. It does take a long time to cook oat groats, but you can throw this together the night before and set it to cook in the morning.

Make in a 3-quart or 6-quart (3-L or 6-L) Instant Pot. Double and make in your 8-quart (8-L) Instant Pot.

SOY-FREE. OIL-FREE. REFINED SUGAR-FREE OPTION

Makes 8 servings

PRESSURE COOKER INGREDIENTS

3 cups (708 ml) water

2 cups (336 g) oat groats, rinsed and drained

2 cups (266 g) chopped sweet potatoes

2 tsp (4 g) ground cinnamon

1 tsp ground ginger

¾ tsp ground allspice

⅛ tsp ground cloves

TOPPINGS (OPTIONAL)

Sweetener of choice, to taste (Maple or date syrup is my favorite.)

Toasted pecans

Toasted coconut

Chopped dates

Add the water, oat groats, sweet potatoes, cinnamon, ginger, allspice and cloves to your Instant Pot. Cook on high pressure for 60 minutes. Manually release the pressure. Mash the sweet potatoes with a potato masher. The oat groats should still stay whole.

Serve with your favorite toppings (if using). You can freeze extra servings for a grab-and-go breakfast another time.

This recipe is the perfect one to use the Instant Pot delay timer. Add the pressure cooker ingredients to your Instant Pot and seal. Select manual and set the time to 60 minutes. Then click the timer button and adjust the time to the amount you want it to wait to start cooking. For example, you'll set it for 8 hours if you want it to start to cook 8 hours from when you set it.

NOTE: The timer will count down until it's time to begin cooking.

PER SERVING: Calories 114.9, protein 4.0 g, total fat 1.6 g, carbohydrates 22.1 g, sodium 4.3 mg, fiber 8.0 g

Ashley's Dark Chocolate Quinoa Porridge

SOY-FREE. OIL-FREE.
REFINED SUGAR-FREE

Makes 4 servings

My friend Ashley (@plantcenteredprep) is a plant-based dietitian and is the queen of meal prep. When she told me about this chocolate breakfast recipe, I knew I had to share it with you. It's creamy, coconutty and can be topped with fruit, nuts and more. You can make it different every day you eat it!

Make in a 3-quart or 6-quart (3-L or 6-L) Instant Pot. Double and make in your 8-quart (8-L) Instant Pot.

PRESSURE COOKER INGREDIENTS

1½ cups (255 g) quinoa, rinsed and drained

1 (13.5-oz [400-ml]) can full-fat coconut milk

1½ cups (355 ml) unsweetened nondairy milk

¼ cup (25 g) cacao or cocoa powder (use less for a lighter chocolate flavor)

¼ cup (59 ml) maple syrup, date syrup or sweetener of choice, or to taste

TOPPINGS (OPTIONAL)

Fresh strawberries and raspberries

Cacao nibs

Shredded coconut

Coconut whip

Add the quinoa, coconut milk, nondairy milk, cacao powder and syrup to your Instant Pot. Mix well to combine. Cook on high pressure for 8 minutes. Manually release the pressure. Mix well.

Portion out into meal prep containers and add your favorite toppings (if using). You can also wait and add the toppings when you are ready to serve.

The cooked and prepped porridge will last in the fridge for up to 5 days. Follow Ashley's suggestion: Make this on a Sunday to have breakfast ready for most of the week.

PER SERVING: Calories 499.3, protein 11.7 g, total fat 27.7 g, carbohydrates 66.8 g, sodium 94.8 mg, fiber 11.9 g

desserts and drinks

I love a little sweet after dinner, and these drinks and desserts fit the bill. In this chapter, you'll find a Creamy Corn Cinnamon Drink (Atole) (page 152) and a ginger turmeric tea (page 155) to settle your stomach. Don't worry, there are also rich puddings and even cakes for you to make for treats. There are refined sugar–free options, too.

Creamy Corn Cinnamon Drink (Atole)

SOY-FREE. OIL-FREE OPTION. REFINED SUGAR-FREE OPTION

Makes 6 servings

This drink is usually served warm, but I drink it chilled in the summer. Either way, a little cup is a perfect drinkable dessert after a nice Mexican dinner. I didn't think a corn drink could taste *this amazing*—but it does!

Make in a 3-quart or 6-quart (3-L or 6-L) Instant Pot. Double and make in your 8-quart (8-L) Instant Pot.

PRESSURE COOKER INGREDIENTS

3 cups (708 ml) water

2 cups (330 g) corn kernels (Fresh is best, but frozen will work, too.)

¼ cup (38 g) raw cashews

2 whole cinnamon sticks

AFTER COOKING INGREDIENTS

¼–½ cup (50–100 g) brown sugar or sweetener of choice, to taste

Add the water, corn, cashews and cinnamon sticks to your Instant Pot liner. Set the Instant Pot to manual/pressure cook and cook on high pressure for 15 minutes. Let the pressure release naturally for 10 minutes, then release the rest of the pressure manually.

Remove the cinnamon sticks. Use either a blender or an immersion blender to puree all the ingredients. Add the sweetener, to taste, while it's still hot. If you are using really sweet corn, you may not need much sweetener at all!

You can also make this into ice cream by adding the chilled atole to your ice cream maker. Follow your maker's instructions. Or take the easy way out and make popsicles!

Make this nut-free by adding an additional ½ cup (88 g) of corn kernels in place of the cashews. You can add a little nondairy milk if you feel it's not creamy enough as is.

PER SERVING: Calories 83.0, protein 2.6 g, total fat 2.8 g, carbohydrates 14.2 g, sodium 2.7 mg, fiber 1.9 g

Fresh Turmeric Ginger Tea Concentrate

SOY-FREE. OIL-FREE. REFINED SUGAR-FREE OPTION

Makes 6 servings (about ½ cup [118 ml] concentrate)

We all know that ginger turmeric tea is good for inflammation and a good tummy tamer. But did you know it's tasty, too? This spicy and healthy drink is a great way to start your day.

Make in a 3-quart, 6-quart or 8-quart (3-L, 6-L or 8-L) Instant Pot.

PRESSURE COOKER INGREDIENTS

2-inch (5-cm) piece fresh turmeric root, sliced thin or shredded

2-inch (5-cm) piece fresh ginger, peeled and chopped

9 whole cardamom pods

3 whole cinnamon sticks

6 whole black peppercorns

3 cups (708 ml) water

AFTER COOKING INGREDIENTS

Sweetener of choice, to taste (Maple syrup and date syrup are my favorites.)

NOTE: Fresh turmeric will turn your hands yellow, so be sure to wear gloves if that bothers you.

Add the turmeric, ginger, cardamom, cinnamon, peppercorns and water to your Instant Pot. Cook on high pressure for 5 minutes and let the pressure release naturally.

Strain through a fine-mesh strainer. Add the sweetener and mix well. Note: This is a concentrate and you will want to make it sweeter than you want your final drink to be.

Store in the fridge for up to 1 week.

To serve: Mix ½ cup (118 ml) of concentrate with your favorite nondairy milk. I use a 70/30 ratio, but make it the way you like it. Heat the mixture on the stove in a pan or in a mug in your microwave.

Want to drink this every morning? Make a double or triple batch, depending on how much your Instant Pot will hold. You can freeze it in ice cube trays or in the amount you will use in a week. Thaw and enjoy!

PER SERVING (DOES NOT INCLUDE SWEETENER): Calories 4.6, protein 0.1 g, total fat 0.9 g, carbohydrates 1.5 g, sodium 1.1 mg, fiber 0.0 g

Rosewater Kheer

Kheer is an Indian spiced rice pudding. This version is an extra creamy, rich rice pudding that's full of nuts and raisins with just a hint of rosewater. It is the perfect decadent dessert to serve your nonvegan friends or relatives. If you're a rosewater fan like me, double the amount.

SOY-FREE, OIL-FREE, REFINED SUGAR-FREE OPTION

Makes 4 servings

Make in a 3-quart or 6-quart (3-L or 6-L) Instant Pot. Double and make in your 8-quart (8-L) Instant Pot.

PRESSURE COOKER INGREDIENTS

2 cups (475 ml) water

1 (13.5-oz [400-ml]) can full-fat coconut milk

½ cup (98 g) white basmati rice

½ cup (100 g) vegan sugar

½ cup (55 g) sliced almonds or chopped cashews

½ cup (75 g) golden raisins

7 cardamom pods

Pinch of saffron

BEFORE SERVING

½ tsp rosewater

Add the water, coconut milk, rice, sugar, almonds, raisins, cardamom pods and saffron to your Instant Pot. Cook on high pressure for 15 minutes. Manually release the pressure.

Stir in the rosewater, and serve this pudding hot or cold.

Make this without sugar by leaving it out during cooking. Then add the sweetener of your choice, to taste, when the cooking time is complete.

PER SERVING: Calories 524.7, protein 31.3 g, total fat 30.7 g, carbohydrates 60.0 g, sodium 57.2 mg, fiber 2.7 g

Almond Berry Cake

You need a nice dessert that's easy to put together and doesn't heat up the house on those hot summer days. You can use any berries that are in season in this. Serve it topped with a scoop of vegan ice cream, or cut it into cubes and layer it with coconut whipped cream and more fresh berries to make it into a mini trifle.

Make in a 6-quart or 8-quart (6-L or 8-L) Instant Pot.

SOY-FREE. OIL-FREE

Makes 6 servings

WET INGREDIENTS

1 cup (236 ml) nondairy milk

1 tsp apple cider vinegar

1 tsp almond extract

DRY INGREDIENTS

1½ cups (180 g) gluten-free baking mix

½ cup (100 g) vegan sugar

1 tbsp (7 g) ground flaxseed

½ tsp baking powder

½ tsp baking soda

⅛ tsp salt

SEASONAL FRUIT

1 cup (150 g) blueberries, raspberries, blackberries, cherries or combination

NOTE: For this recipe, I use a 7-inch (18-cm) stainless steel pan with a removable bottom that even has a handle.

Oil a pan that fits into your Instant Pot or cover in parchment paper to keep oil-free. In a large measuring cup, combine the nondairy milk, vinegar and almond extract.

In a small mixing bowl, combine the baking mix, sugar, ground flaxseed, baking powder, baking soda and salt.

Add the wet mix to the dry one. Stir well. Pour one-half of the batter in the prepared pan and spread it evenly. Layer on the fruit. Pour in the rest of the batter and spread evenly. Cover with foil.

Add the rack to your Instant Pot and add 1½ cups (355 ml) of water. Cook on high pressure for 35 minutes. Let the pressure release naturally.

The top may be cracked a bit, but you can cover that up with ice cream or vegan whipped cream.

To make handles out of aluminum foil: Tear off two pieces of foil about 3 feet (1 m) long, fold each one lengthwise two times. Lay the foil handles out on the counter in a plus sign near your cooker. Place your pan or container in the center, where the two pieces cross. Pull the handles up and carefully lift the pan or container into your Instant Pot.

PER SERVING: Calories 200.0, protein 2.1 g, total fat 1.2 g, carbohydrates 46.4 g, sodium 235.1 mg, fiber 2.7 g

No Sugar Dessert Hummus 2 Ways

I know, dessert hummus may not sound exciting—but stay with me. In this recipe we're using beans to make up the bulk of our dip, then adding dates and vanilla to give it that caramel goodness. My favorite way to make this is to add in some cocoa powder to about half of the hummus and use it as a Nutella-like spread. I serve it with caramel dip, seasonal fresh fruit and gluten-free bread for a fun dessert tray.

Make in a 3-quart or 6-quart (3-L or 6-L) Instant Pot.

PRESSURE COOKER INGREDIENTS

2 cups (475 ml) water

1½ cups (220 g) chopped dates

1 cup (200 g) channa dal

AFTER COOKING INGREDIENTS

2 tsp (10 ml) vanilla extract

Salt, to taste (optional)

Sweetener of choice, to taste (optional)

¼ cup (25 g) cocoa or cacao powder (optional; use to make both dips)

Nondairy milk, as needed

Add the water, dates and channa dal to your Instant Pot. Cook on high pressure for 18 minutes. Release the pressure manually.

Add the vanilla. Use either a blender or an immersion blender to puree all the ingredients.

Taste and add some salt (if using) to bring out the sweet taste a bit more. If it's not sweet enough, add a little of your favorite sweetener until it's just the way you like it.

If you want to make the second dip: Remove one-half of the mixture. Add the cocoa and blend again until smooth. If you are using a blender, you may need to add some nondairy milk if the mixture is too thick to blend well.

Channa dal is a baby chickpea that's been skinned and split. They are used a lot in Indian cuisine. You can get them at Indian markets or order online from Amazon. You can substitute 1 cup (200 g) of dried chickpeas instead if that's what you have in your pantry. Just be sure to up the cooking time to 45 minutes.

PER SERVING: Calories 98.5, protein 3.4 g, total fat 1.1 g, carbohydrates 20.8 g, sodium 3.6 mg, fiber 3.9 g

Carrot Cake Sweetened with Dates

SOY-FREE. OIL-FREE. REFINED SUGAR-FREE

Makes 12 servings

My Instant Pot carrot cake is sweetened with dates instead of refined sugar, and the cooking method keeps it moist even though it's oil-free! Keep in mind that gluten-free baking blends are all so different that you may have to tweak the liquid or flour amount a little.

Make in a 6-quart or 8-quart (6-L or 8-L) Instant Pot.

1½ cups (180 g) gluten-free baking blend

¾ tsp baking powder

¾ tsp baking soda

½ tsp ground cinnamon

¼ tsp ground cardamom

¼ tsp ground allspice

¼ tsp ground ginger

¼ tsp salt

2 tbsp (18 g) ground flaxseed, mixed with ¼ cup (59 ml) warm water

1 cup (236 ml) nondairy milk

¼ cup (57 g) mashed ripe avocado

½ tsp orange flower water or vanilla extract

1 cup (110 g) shredded carrot

1 cup (147 g) chopped dates

FOR THE ICING

½ cup (75 g) cashews

½ cup (74 g) chopped dates

½ cup (118 ml) water, plus more as needed

1½ tsp (8 ml) orange flower water

Add 1½ cups (355 ml) of water to your Instant Pot liner and then put your rack in it. This will keep the pan above the water.

Prepare a pan that fits into your 6-quart (6-L) or 8-quart (8-L) Instant Pot. Spray the pan with oil and/or line with parchment paper.

In a large mixing bowl, mix the baking blend, baking powder, baking soda, cinnamon, cardamom, allspice, ginger and salt.

In a smaller bowl, mix the flaxseed, nondairy milk, avocado and orange flower water. Add the carrot and dates. Mix well.

Add the wet mixture to the dry mixture. Spread the batter in the prepared pan. Cover with aluminum foil and seal well so water will not get in. Place the covered pan on the rack in your Instant Pot. Cook on high pressure for 50 minutes. Let the pressure release naturally.

While the cake cooks, make the icing: Place the cashews, dates, water and orange flower water into a saucepan and bring to a boil. Take the pan off the heat and let it cool. Take the cooled mixture and put it in a small blender. Blend until smooth and add extra water if needed.

The cake may have some cracks on the top, but don't worry—you'll cover that up with the icing. Let the cake cool before icing it.

Mango Cardamom Tapioca Pudding

This is a rich dessert that's perfect to bring to parties where you're introducing vegan food. Just make this pudding a day before and let it chill in the fridge until you're ready to go.

Make in a 3-quart, 6-quart or 8-quart (3-L, 6-L or 8-L) Instant Pot. Follow the specific size notes in the recipe directions.

SOY-FREE, OIL-FREE,
REFINED SUGAR-FREE
OPTION

Makes 4 servings

PRESSURE COOKER INGREDIENTS

1 (13.5-oz [400-ml]) can full-fat coconut milk

½ cup (88 g) small tapioca pearls (not quick-cooking)

2 cups (330 g) mango chunks, cut small or diced

½ cup (118 ml) water

1 tsp ground cardamom

AFTER COOKING INGREDIENTS

Sweetener of choice, to taste (optional; only if needed)

Add water to the bottom of your electric pressure cooker liner. In a Pyrex or stainless steel bowl that fits into your electric pressure cooker, add the coconut milk, tapioca, mango, water and cardamom. Whisk until thoroughly combined.

Cover the bowl with foil. You can lower the bowl down using the rack that came with your Instant Pot. I also recommend using an OXO sling or making handles out of aluminum foil (page 159) to make it easier to get it out later.

Cook on high pressure for 20 minutes. Release the pressure naturally for 5 minutes, then manually release the rest of the pressure. Remove the bowl from the electric pressure cooker and set it on a trivet.

The pudding will be liquid at this point. Don't worry, it will get firm and set up after it's refrigerated for a few hours.

Taste the pudding. If the mangos you used are very ripe you will not need any additional sweetener. If it's not sweet enough for you, stir in the sweetener of your choice until it's the way you like it. Do this before the pudding is completely cool to ensure that the sweetener gets totally combined.

Transfer the pudding to single-serving cups if you like. Chill the pudding in the refrigerator for at least 2 hours before serving.

If you avoid canned coconut milk, you can use your choice of nondairy milk instead.

PER SERVING: Calories 828.6, protein 4.0 g, total fat 17.2 g, carbohydrates 33.0 g, sodium 1.7 mg, fiber 1.5 g

Appendix

BEAN COOKING CHART

QUICK-COOKING BEANS/LENTILS

No soaking is required for these beans and lentils. If you choose to soak them, cut the cook time in half.

- Beluga Lentils: 4–6 minutes

- Green French Lentils: 5–7 minutes

- Brown Lentils: 6–8 minutes

- Red Lentils: 4–6 minutes

- Split Peas: 5–8 minutes

IN-BETWEEN COOKING BEANS

These beans don't really require soaking and typically cook on the stove for 30 minutes to 1 hour.

BEANS	SOAKED	UNSOAKED
Adzuki Beans	6–9 minutes	15–20 minutes
Black-Eyed Peas	3–5 minutes	7–9 minutes
Cranberry Beans	7–9 minutes	20–25 minutes
Lima Beans	7–9 minutes	20–25 minutes
Navy Beans	5–8 minutes	15–20 minutes
Pinto Beans	4–6 minutes	15–20 minutes

LONG-COOKING BEANS

These beans can take as long as 4 hours when cooked on the stove, so you are saving a ton of time whether you soak or not!

BEANS	SOAKED	UNSOAKED
Cannellini Beans	9–11 minutes	22–27 minutes
Black Beans	9–11 minutes	22–27 minutes
Chickpeas	12–15 minutes	35–45 minutes
Kidney Beans	9–11 minutes	22–27 minutes
Soybeans	18–23 minutes	40–45 minutes

Older beans may require longer cooking times. If the beans are not cooked in the time specified, just replace the lid and cook 5 to 10 minutes more.

VEGETABLE COOKING CHART

LONG-COOKING VEGETABLES

Instant Pots are great for cutting down the time it takes to cook vegetables. I find that long-cooking vegetables are great to layer on the bottom of the Instant Pot. Use high pressure unless otherwise noted.

- Beets, medium, whole: 15 minutes

- White Baking Potato, medium, whole: 15 minutes

- Baby Potatoes, whole: 10 minutes

- Turnips, whole: 8 minutes

- Sweet Potatoes, medium, whole: 15 minutes

- Winter Squash, medium, whole: 15 minutes

QUICK-COOKING VEGETABLES

Cooking times will vary depending on age, thickness and other factors, but here are a few starting points for quick-cooking vegetables. Use high pressure unless otherwise noted.

- Asparagus, medium, whole: 1 minute

- Broccoli, florets: 2 minutes

- Brussels Sprouts, baby: 2 minutes

- Brussels Sprouts, large: 3 minutes

- Carrots, sliced: 2 minutes

- Cauliflower, florets: 2 minutes

- Green Beans, whole or half: 2 minutes

- Greens, whole or chopped: 2 minutes

- Peas, medium, whole: 2 minutes

- Summer Squash, medium, whole: 0 minutes

GRAIN COOKING CHART

Different kinds of grains weigh vastly different amounts. Make sure you measure by volume, not weight.

QUICK-COOKING GRAINS

- Amaranth, 5 minutes: 2¼ cups (530 ml) liquid
- Millet, 10 minutes: 1½ cups (355 ml) liquid
- Quinoa, 3 minutes: 1½ cups (355 ml) liquid
- Rolled Oats (cooked in ramekins inside pressure cooker), 4 minutes: 2 cups (475 ml) liquid
- Sorghum, 35 minutes: 2½ cups (590 ml) liquid
- Steel-Cut Oats, 3 minutes: 3 cups (708 ml) liquid

RICE

- Arborio Rice, 6–8 minutes: 3 cups (708 ml) liquid
- Black Forbidden Rice, 15 minutes: 1½ cups (355 ml) liquid
- Brown Rice, 23 minutes: 1¼ cups (296 ml) liquid
- Sushi Rice, 6 minutes: 1 cup (236 ml) liquid
- White Rice, 4 minutes: 1 cup (236 ml) liquid or use the rice function/ button on the Instant Pot

Natural Pressure Release Vs. Manual or Quick Pressure Release

When you are using a pressure cooker, pressure builds up and that's the reason food cooks faster than with other methods. The pressure will need to be released before you can open the pot.

Remember that you are dealing with piping hot food no matter which release method you use. Always use caution!

NATURAL PRESSURE RELEASE (NPR)

This is when you let the pressure release on its own without doing anything. It's even easier than it sounds!

Once the cooking time is done, the Instant Pot will switch to the warming setting automatically. Once the float valve lowers, the pressure is released and you can open the lid.

QUICK PRESSURE RELEASE (QPR)

To do a quick pressure release, you carefully turn the release valve to manually release the pressure. Pay attention so that no hot liquid gets sprayed on you.

I use a silicone pot holder when I use this method. The end of the rice paddle will work too because it will fit over the lever and will give you some space between your fingers and the hot steam.

You can also buy a vent cover that will allow you to avoid contact with the steam. I have a dragon, and there are so many choices of funny styles. You don't have to have one of these, but the dragon puts on a good show.

If you are cooking a soup or anything with a lot of liquid, open the valve in very short and quick bursts. This will keep any liquid from coming out with the steam.

If you just throw the valve all the way open eventually the liquid will start coming out and make a mess. Just remember the short bursts.

10-MINUTE RELEASE

Wait until the cook cycle has completed, then wait until the keep-warm cycle counts up to 10 minutes. It's safer to move the pressure valve and you may get to eat a few minutes sooner.

Keep in mind, you may still have to move the pressure valve for short bursts if it's a soup or a dish with lots of liquid.

If I'm not sure what kind of release to do, the 10-minute release is my go-to.

HOW TO DECIDE WHAT PRESSURE RELEASE METHOD TO USE

Most of the time a recipe will tell you what method of pressure release is best. There are a few things you should know to make the right choice in your own recipe experimentations.

NPR is good for beans that you want extra creamy and things that you aren't afraid of overcooking. So that means you do not want to use it for delicate things that could overcook easily.

Recipes that use natural pressure release are also using that time for extra cooking. If you open it sooner, it may not be quite done.

MPR/QPR is great for delicate things that could overcook such as pasta, broccoli or the like.

Must-Have Accessories

This book uses a few accessories that don't come with your Instant Pot. You will find the links to all of them here: https://plantbasedinstantpot.com/glutenfreeveganbook.

The most important ones to have are the following:

- A silicone egg mold for muffins and corn dogs
- A 7-inch (18-cm) stainless steel pan with a removable bottom
- A stainless steel rack with 2- to 3-inch (5- to 7.5-cm) legs
- An oven-safe container that fits on the rack and holds about 5 cups of food

I'm also a huge fan of the OXO pressure cooker bakeware sling. It's reusable and is the perfect tool to lower and raise a pan or container.

Taking Good Care of Your Instant Pot

Your electric pressure cooker can do a ton, but unfortunately it can't clean itself. In addition to learning how to take care of your Instant Pot, you should go ahead and get extra silicone sealing rings.

SILICONE SEALING RING

The gasket or silicone sealing ring that seals your Instant Pot will need to be replaced about every year. If the pot is having trouble getting up to pressure on recipes it has done fine with in the past, it may be a sign to replace it. If it has any cracks or splits it must be replaced immediately.

You will probably want to have an extra one on hand. The ring also absorbs strong smells, and having a spare can keep your yogurt from smelling like curry. You can remove the sealing ring from the lid, so you can wash and dry it thoroughly to help keep it odor-free. You can wash this by hand or in the dishwasher.

Also, storing the lid ring side up will help odors dissipate. Some people recommend taking it out and letting it sit in the sun for a day to remove odors.

STEAM RELEASE VALVE

This is on the top of the lid and is what you move to seal or to release steam. It will pop off and you can wash it and check to make sure nothing is blocking it.

ANTI-BLOCK SHIELD

This little stainless steel "cage" protects the Instant Pot from clogging. It also comes off to be cleaned as well.

CONDENSATION COLLECTOR

This little plastic condensation collector is on the upper back of the Instant Pot base. It's made of plastic and can be removed for dumping and cleaning. It mainly collects runoff when you place the lid in the side-lid holder on the top of the base.

INNER STAINLESS STEEL POT

This can be washed by hand or even in the dishwasher. I find that if you have stuck-on or burnt food on the bottom, soaking overnight with water and dishwashing liquid will make it much easier to clean.

THE OUTSIDE

Never immerse the outside pot in water because that's where its electrical components are housed. Unplug the unit and clean with a damp cloth, then dry immediately.

SLOW COOKING IN YOUR INSTANT POT

There is a slow cooking function and I do use it. However, there are recipes in this book that are not a fit. I do not recommend using the slow cooker setting to cook dry beans or to bake desserts in. You can still use your Instant Pot, just use the pressure cooker settings for those recipes instead.

Answers for Beginners

Q: HOW CAN I TELL WHEN THE INSTANT POT HAS COME UP TO PRESSURE?

Some electric pressure cookers make it easier than others to tell if they have come up to pressure. I've noticed that later Instant Pot models and Mealthy models have a red float valve that is easy to see when it pops up. In fact, those also pop up above the hole they are in to make it crystal clear.

On other pressure cookers the float valve is solid silver metal and comes up flush with the lid when it's up to pressure and that's pretty easy to see.

The hardest ones to tell is on the Lux models of Instant Pot. The float valve is hollow—without a solid top—and that makes it harder to see.

The easiest way to get a good idea of what you need to look for is to turn the lid upside down over your head. Gravity will extend the float valve to its full extension, so you can see exactly how it will look.

Then turn it over to see it in the lowest point. Go back and forth like that until you have a good feel for how your Instant Pot will look.

Q: HOW CAN I TELL WHEN THE INSTANT POT HAS FINISHED A COOKING CYCLE?

The Instant Pot will beep and then it will switch to keep warm. If you were gone for the cooking time, look to see which button is lit up.

Q: HOW CAN I TELL WHEN THE INSTANT POT'S PRESSURE HAS BEEN COMPLETELY RELEASED?

First, know that you cannot open the lid unless the pressure is completely released. You can read the first question about how to tell when it's gotten up to pressure and look for the valve to come down.

Sometimes the float valve will stick, especially after many uses. Just touch with a chopstick and it will come down easily if that's the case.

Q: HOW CAN I TELL WHEN THE INSTANT POT IS HEATED UP ON SAUTÉ?

This is the easiest question—the display reads HOT. Most models give you the option to choose less, normal or more as your sauté temperature.

Q: IS THE TIME IT TAKES TO COME UP TO PRESSURE INCLUDED IN THE COOK TIME?

It is not. It can take 10 to 15 minutes for the pressure to build up. At that point you will see the screen indicate how many minutes it has been cooking.

Q: DO I ALWAYS HAVE TO ADD WATER OR LIQUID TO MY INSTANT POT?

You do if you want to use the pressure cooker function, the steam function or any of the buttons that use the pressure cooker function.

Note that your manual will state the minimum amount of liquid you need for your size and model.

It's actually easier to tell you that you don't need to add liquid for the yogurt or sauté functions. For everything else, check the manual and add the amount of liquid needed.

Q: I'M DOUBLING A RECIPE. DO I NEED TO DOUBLE THE COOKING TIME TOO?

Nope. The cooking time should remain the same—even if you cut a recipe in half or double a recipe.

Q: MY STEAM RELEASE VALVE IS LOOSE AND EVEN COMES OFF. IS THERE SOMETHING WRONG WITH IT?

That's just the way it's supposed to be. It will easily go from venting to sealing and can even be taken off for cleaning. Make sure when you take it off that the pointer is facing the correct direction when you put it back on. Refer to your manual to double-check.

Q: I'M STILL SCARED TO GET MY INSTANT POT OUT OF THE BOX. IS THERE A VIDEO OR CLASS THAT I CAN WATCH?

There sure is! If you want you can watch me make chai in a video on my blog, go here: https://plantbasedinstantpot.com/instant-pot-chai-tea-concentrate/

I also have online electric pressure cooking and other vegan cooking classes that you can take here: https://kathy-hester.teachable.com/courses

General Instant Pot Dos and Don'ts

Always read your manual: there are important updated details about your model of Instant Pot in there. You can always get a copy online at: http://instantpot.com/benefits/specifications-and-manuals

Never leave any appliance alone the first time you cook in it! It could be defective and cause problems. After your first test run, you can take the dog for a walk, read or generally ignore it while it's cooking your dinner.

Never cook with a dry pressure cooker—it needs liquid to come up to pressure. Also note that if you cook something a second time using a steaming method you will probably have to add more water in the bottom before you recook it.

Never overfill the pot. Remember that beans and grains will expand up to twice their size while cooking.

Cooking times are not written in stone and one bag of dried pinto beans may take a couple of minutes longer to cook than another. You can always put the lid back on and cook a few minutes longer. Remember, the beans are the variable.

Never attempt to force the lid open on your pressure cooker. If it won't open, that means the pressure has not released. It's very dangerous to force the lid!

Never try to pressure can in your cooker; the temperature of the pressure does not get high enough to safely can. Instead, you'll need to buy a stovetop canning pressure cooker.

Make sure the outside of the stainless steel inner liner is completely dry before you put it in the base.

Always double-check that the liner is in the cooker before you pour in ingredients. I always push the base under my cabinets as a signal that it needs the insert. When I pull out the base I always see the inside, so I won't be tempted to pour water in without looking first.

Always wash the lid well after cooking and empty the plastic condensation collector that is on the top back of the pressure cooker.

Live in a high altitude? "Cooking time under pressure should be increased by 5 percent for every 1,000 feet after 2,000 feet above sea level." – B. M. Anderson, *The New High Altitude Cookbook*. (1980)

Always check the pressure release valve to make sure it's clear. Do this each time before using.

Never immerse the cord or the outside of the Instant Pot in water. Clean with a damp cloth if needed.

Remember, the outside will get hot, so keep the Instant Pot out of the reach of children and pets. Also keep plastics and other things that could melt away from the base.

Do not store your Instant Pot on your stove—there are many horror stories of melting Instant Pots and ruined stove burners.

After cleaning, always store the stainless steel liner in the base. That way you will never accidentally pour ingredients directly into the base.

Troubleshooting

MY INSTANT POT IS NOT SEALING

These are the most common reasons why an Instant Pot won't seal.

- The pressure valve is set to venting.
- There is an issue with the sealing ring.
- There is not enough liquid to bring the pot up to pressure.
- Food is scorched on the bottom of the pot.
- The pot is too full.
- There is too much liquid.
- The lid has debris or dirt that is causing a leak.
- There is debris on the rim of the inner stainless steel pot.

STEAM IS COMING OUT ALL AROUND THE LID

If steam is coming out all around the lid of your Instant Pot, follow these steps:

- Check to make sure the lid is all the way closed and locked.
- Check the sealing ring: Make sure it's in place in the lid. Check for any debris. Clean the ring if debris is found.
- Try to push the ring back into place: If it's stretched or cracked, you will need to replace it. If it's just a little loose, place the ring in the freezer to tighten it back up a little and you may be able to use it a few more times.

STEAM IS LEAKING FROM THE FLOAT VALVE

Some steam will leak from the float valve while it's building up pressure. In fact, if you have a Mealthy brand it does this for longer than the other brands.

If steam leaks are happening all the time, the anti-block shield on the underside of the lid may be dirty or sticking. Check to be sure the pressure brings up the float valve. When in doubt, give your lid a good cleaning and see if that does the trick. You can also remove the anti-block shield, and you may need to do that to identify the source of the problem.

Remember you can put the whole lid in the dishwasher on the top rack. This helps keep it clean and free of obstructions.

STEAM LEAKING FROM THE STEAM RELEASE HANDLE

If the steam release handle is not there, put it on. If it is on, make sure that it's facing the right way. You can do that by looking in your manual or looking it up on Google.

THE FLOAT VALVE NOT COMING UP OR NOT GOING DOWN

Chances are that the valve is stuck. There is a piece of silicone on the float valve that can wear out over time. But chances are good that it's just debris. Clean the valve and lid well, removing the parts as needed. You can also try cleaning the whole lid in the dishwasher.

I HEAR A POPPING SOUND

Usually this is just a sign that there was water on the inner stainless steel liner when you put it in. The easiest way to avoid this is to thoroughly dry off the outside of the liner before you put it in.

MY SEALING RING SMELLS

This happens. Silicone holds smells. First, I recommend that you have two silicone rings: use one for sweet and the other for savory. To keep smells from building up wash the whole lid—with the sealing ring still attached—in the top rack of your dishwasher.

BURN NOTICE AND OTHER TROUBLESHOOTING CODES

There are many codes that can pop up on your Instant Pot. They vary between models and makes, and I recommend checking your manual for specific codes when they come up.

Here are a few of the more common or crucial ones. Hopefully you'll never see any of these codes—but things happen, so don't panic if you do.

BURN

First, know that your Instant Pot is not on fire! This code shows up particularly on my Ultra; they seem to be more sensitive.

The burn code does mean that food is sticking to the bottom of the liner and probably overcooking. Usually this is caused by having too little liquid in your pot. If you find that the food you're cooking is just too thick, you can switch to sauté and cook it the way you would if it was on the stove. I do this for split pea soup.

Generally, you can fix this issue by adding more liquid and restarting the pressure cooking cycle.

LID

This means your lid is not locked on and that the selected program needs it to be locked.

This error lets you know that your electric pressure cooker cannot reach pressure.

I find that more often than not this error doesn't display. Even without the error message showing, you can tell if your float valve is not up and your screen is still counting minutes of cooking.

This error usually relates to the gasket, so check it first. If that's not the issue, then you may need to add more liquid.

Instant Pot Resources & Recommended Reading

FACEBOOK GROUPS

VEGAN COOKING WITH KATHY HESTER
facebook.com/groups/vegancookingwithkathy

INSTANT POT FOR EAT TO LIVE
facebook.com/groups/360857787663311

INSTANT POT VEGAN RECIPES
facebook.com/groups/InstantPotVeganRecipes

INSTANT POT COMMUNITY (NOT VEGAN)
facebook.com/groups/InstantPotCommunity

PLANT-BASED INSTANT POT PEOPLE
facebook.com/groups/790787064328258

WEBSITES AND BLOGS

VEGAN PRESSURE COOKER
plantbasedinstantpot.com

healthyslowcooking.com

fatfreevegan.com

glueandglitter.com

theveggiequeen.com

VEGAN BLOGS
healthiersteps.com

plantcenteredprep.com

veggiessavetheday.com

chefajwebsite.com

NONVEGAN BLOGS
simplyvegetarian777.com

simmertoslimmer.com

nanciemcdermott.com

NONVEGAN PRESSURE COOKER
hippressurecooking.com

pressurecookingtoday.com

twosleevers.com

OTHER COOKBOOKS
Vegan Under Pressure by Jill Nussinow

O M Gee Good! Instant Pot Meals, Plant-Based & Oil-Free by Jill McKeever

The New Fast Food by Jill Nussinow

Hip Pressure Cooking by Laura D.A. Pazzaglia

Great Vegetarian Cooking Under Pressure by Lorna J. Sass

Vegetarian Indian Cooking with Your Instant Pot by Manali Singh

Acknowledgments

I love working with Page Street Publishing because of Will Kiester and Marissa Giambelluca.

Lisa and Sally Ekus are the best agents a girl could ever hope for and were a wonderful support throughout the whole process of this book. Thank you all so much for believing in my vision.

I have so much gratitude for my testers' help and guidance. You make this book better than I ever could alone.

Many thanks to Marissa Giambelluca for doing an amazing editing job, along with the best copy editor ever Jenna Nelson Patton. You guys make sure that everything is crystal clear for the readers.

I always love Kylie Alexander's wonderful layouts, and this book is no exception.

Many thanks to Cheryl Purser and my friends who didn't get mad at me when I went into "book mode" yet again. I think it's time for a big vacation all together!

About the Author

Kathy Hester is the author of *Vegan Cooking in Your Air Fryer*, *The Easy Vegan Cookbook*, *The Great Vegan Bean Book* and the bestselling *The Ultimate Vegan Cookbook for Your Instant Pot®*.

She's the blogger behind HealthySlowCooking.com, does freelance writing, food styling, food photography and recipe development, and teaches people just how easy it is to cook in her online cooking classes.

When she's not writing or being a mad scientist in the kitchen, she's probably drinking tea on the deck while reading *Harry Potter* one more time.

She lives in Durham, North Carolina, with a grown-up picky eater, two quirky dogs and one crazy cat.

Index